Stacks

THE COLLECTED POEMS OF

WILLIAM ALEXANDER PERCY

Also by WILLIAM ALEXANDER PERCY

LANTERNS

ON THE LEVEE

Recollections of a Planter's Son

"The deep South, the old South, a New South, several Souths, move across Will Percy's autobiography. If the writing of one who has learned the craft counts, if candor and honesty and forthright confession count, if a heart and mind haunted by some of the most ancient issues of justice and charity count, this rates among the autobiographies requisite to understanding America."

—CARL SANDBURG

PUBLISHED BY ALFRED A. KNOPF

The Collected Poems of

WILLIAM ALEXANDER

PERCY

Foreword by ROARK BRADFORD

1943 Alfred A. Knopf NEW YORK

THIS BOOK HAS BEEN PRODUCED IN FULL COMPLIANCE WITH ALL GOVERNMENT REGULATIONS FOR THE CONSERVATION OF PAPER, METAL, AND OTHER ESSENTIAL MATERIALS.

Copyright 1915, 1920, 1924, 1930, 1943 by LeRoy Pratt Percy, executor of the Estate of William Alexander Percy, deceased. All rights reserved. No part of this book may be reproduced in any form without permission in writing from the publisher, except by a reviewer who may quote brief passages in a review to be printed in a magazine or newspaper.

Manufactured in the United States of America
Published simultaneously in Canada by The Ryerson Press
First Edition

Contents

Foreword   3

Part I. Sappho in Levkas, and Other Poems

Song	11
Sappho in Levkas	12
Chorus	29
To a Mocking-bird	30
All Soul's Day	32
A Page's Road Song	34
Soaring	35
For Music	36
Autumn Tune	37
A Sea-bird	38
Ecstasy	39
In an Autumn Wood	40
Prison Song	41
The Return of the Leaves	41
March Magic	42
St. Francis to the Birds	43
Arcady Lost	54
On Leaving Taormina	55
Dusk: Assuan	56
The Coast of Bohemia	57
To the Mississippi	58
In Dalmatia	59

Invocation	60
To Chatterton	61
The Silent Singers	62
Wild Geese	63
Failure	64
Ex Ætate	65
To Milton	65
To Lucrezia	66
A Page Sings	69
Winter-fear	70
To a Mocking-bird: from Taormina	71
After Reading the Rubaiyat	72
A Winter's Night	73
At Parting	74
Before Dawn	75
Longing	76
Phaon in Hades	78
Girgenti	79
The Happy Isles	83
Epilogue	86

PART II. IN APRIL ONCE, AND OTHER POEMS

I. SICILIANA

In April Once	91
New Moon	129
Where Ilium Was Proud	130
Euripides	131
Farewell to Etna	132
The Immortal Residue	133
Set of Moon	135

II. LYRICAL PIECES

Overtones	139
In New York: 1. *On Sunday Morning*	140
2. *The Song You Love*	140
3. *Weariness*	141
4. *In the Night*	142
5. *Home*	142
The Wanderer	144
The Man in White	146
The Wood	148
In the Storm	149
Mr. W. H. to the Poet	150
November	151
Prologue	152
To an Old Tune	153
A Hunger Song	154
Defeat	155
Lullaby	156
Sanctuary	157
Autumnal	159
A Sea Ballad	160
Australia in London	161
In Our Yard	164
A Wood Song	165
The Little Shepherd's Song	166
Adventure	167
To Butterfly	168
Agricolæ	169
Riolama	170
A Ballad of St. Sebastien	171
The Question	174
Evening Lines	175

III. FROM A SOLDIER'S NOTEBOOK

A Volunteer's Grave	179
Night off Gallipoli: 1. *A Delirious Voice*	180
2. *Voice of a Youthful Turk*	180
3. *An English Voice*	181
4. *Voice of a Breton Fisherman*	182
5. *Voice of an English Poet*	182
6. *A Canadian Voice*	183
7. *Voice of a French Poet*	184
8. *A Host of Spirits*	185
Swallows	187
Poppy Fields	188
On Leave	189
To C. P.	190
In France	191
The Soldier Generation	192
After Any Battle	194
The Squire	195
For Them That Died in Battle	196
The Farm Again	197
An Epistle from Corinth	199

PART III. ENZIO'S KINGDOM, AND OTHER POEMS

I. LYRICS

October	207
A Canticle	208
To One Dying	210
Courage	211
His Peace	212
Hymn of the Magdalene	213

Beth Marie	214
Autumn Song	215
For a Word	216
Safe Secrets	217
Youth	218
Sight and Sound	219
She Grieves in the Dusk	220
Afterglow	221
The Unloved to His Beloved	222
A Mad Maid's Song	223
Exchange	224
A Debussy Serenade	225
Winds of Winter	226
Hymn to the Sun	227
Compensation	228
That Kingdom	229
Autumn Wisdom	230
One Path	232
To a Stranger	233
Wonder and a Thousand Springs	234
Calypso to Ulysses	235
Spring Night in the Mountains	237
Siren Song	238
A Letter	240
After Hearing Music	241
In the Cold Bright Wind	242
The Green Bird Seeth Iseult	243
Avernel	245
Canopus	246
French Blue	248
For a Poet's Birthday	249

A Portrait	250
Rain Patter	251
Meditating a Journey	253
Italian Summer	254
Delight	255
Advice in Springtime	256
Insomnia	257
Sublimation	258
Four Capri Impromptus	259
An Arcadian Idyll	262
A Brittany Idyll	265

II. DELTA SKETCHES

In the Delta		273
Greenville Trees:	*The Lombardy Poplars*	275
	The China-Berries	276
	The Locusts	277
	The Water Oaks	278
The Holy Women		281
A Burnished Calm		282
Levee Nocturne		283
A Memory		284
Song		286
Outcast		287
The Delta Autumn		288

III

A Letter from John Keats to Fanny Brawne	291

IV

Enzio's Kingdom	301
Epilogue	343

Part IV. New Poems

Confidants	347
Recognition	348
Three April Nocturnes: 1. *The Breeze*	349
2. *The Mocking-birds*	349
3. *The Rain*	350
Stirrup Cup	351
At Sea	352
Hill-Top by the Sea	353
Fourteen Sonnets	354
Promethean	362
Trees	363
Certain Casuals	364
Song	364
To a Dogwood in Summer	365
Chimes	366
A Little Hymn	367
L. P.	367
Altitude	368
Pan Rejected	368
Recompense	369
Dirge	369
Shroud Song	370
Threnody	371
For Rip Who Died Mad	372
On a Theme from Sappho	373
At Delphi	373
Three Old Tunes	374
Medusa	376
Cretan Idyl	377

On an Antique Littoral 379
A Legend of Lacedæmon 380
A Regret 386

THE COLLECTED POEMS OF

WILLIAM ALEXANDER PERCY

Foreword

AN INTRODUCTION to the poetry of William Alexander Percy necessarily implies an introduction to the poet himself. I know of no other writer whose work so perceptively expresses his own personality. In his remarkable autobiography, "Lanterns on the Levee," a tour de force written against time and a fatal illness, Will Percy has these cogent words to say of his poetry:

"Since much of my life has gone into the making of verse which I hope is poetry, I may as well state now and as briefly as I can how and why I wrote.

"What I wrote seemed to me more essentially myself than anything I did or said. It often gushed up almost involuntarily like automatic writing, and the difficulty lay in keeping the hot gush continuous and unselfconscious while at the same time directing it with cold intellect into form. I could never write in cold blood. The results were intensely personal, whatever their other defects. . . .

"When you feel something intensely, you want to write it down — if anguish, to stanch the bleeding; if delight, to prolong the moment. When . . . you feel you have discovered a new truth or an old one which suddenly for you has the excitement of a new one, you write a poem. To keep it free from irrelevant photographic details you set it in some long-ago time, one, of course, you love and perhaps once lived in.

"That is how I wrote and why I wrote."

For the last twelve years of his life it was my privilege to know this excellent man. He was physically frail but not weak; he was gentle but not soft. He loved gracious living, beauty, Greece, the song of bird, the smell of rose and the peaceful solitude of his oak-paneled study. Yet he never side-stepped, intellectually or physically, to avoid a fight.

Even before his too-soon death last year, legends began to spread throughout the Mississippi Delta about this small slender man with the shock of gray hair and gray-blue eyes that could warm the spirit of friend or chill the heart of foe. Medals and citations from the Allied governments attest his personal heroism in war. The legends tell of a deadlier kind of bravery from this gentle peaceloving man: Will once sat in the front row at a hostile Ku Klux Klan political meeting where the speaker was scheduled to attack a friend. " The speaker didn't make the attack," the story ends, " so Mr. Will didn't kill him." Countless are the tales of how he bearded local officials, single-handed, and forced them to deal justly with Negroes — neither a trivial nor a popular thing to do in some sections of the State of Mississippi.

Yet this man who walked among the dead and dying in Flanders, and who quenched the fires of fanatical oratory by his mere presence, wrote after a brief visit to New York:

I have need of silence and of stars.
Too much is said too loudly; I am dazed.
The silken sound of whirled infinity
Is lost in voices shouting to be heard.
I once knew men as earnest and less shrill.

He was not alien to his homeland, in spite of seeming always to hold apart from run-of-the-creek Delta cotton and small town lawyer. He had a genuine love of people and the happy genius of attracting loyal friends to himself. Even Mississippi's poor whites, that embittered, underfed, hook-worm-ridden race that thrives on hate and prejudice, regarded him with something between esteem and tolerance. " For a rich man's son, Mr. Will is a right clever man."

Reciprocally, Mr. Will did what he could to understand and to help these people. They represented things he most abhorred — hate, prejudice, disease, shiftlessness, and he strove mightily to bring about an improvement of these people without once deviating from his own high principles.

It is not my purpose to estimate the place in letters Will's poetry occupies. Critics have done that, variously. The only generalities I can apply to it all is that it is beautiful, charming and a delight to read. As the poet's character was complex and seemingly at variance with itself, at times, yet always a pleasure to his friends, always warm with a love for truth and beauty, so is his poetry always warm and honest and lyrical. As he himself was, so is his poetry ever sensitive to though never hysterical about life and death. Often Will withdrew himself from life, not to an ivory tower where the living and the dying world could not touch him, but rather to an Olympus of his own where he could observe with truer perspective and sharper clarity the realities below. What he saw from his Olympus he set down in song.

In " St. Francis to the Birds " we hear the good saint chiding both himself and his winged congregation, though not too seriously:

> *Was ever such a sermon?*
> *I, no text; no morals, you!*

The spirit of the poem is a kind of sly connivance between a not too holy saint and not too evil sinners.

But there is neither tolerance nor gentleness in " An Epistle from Corinth " wherein a Corinthian replies to the letters of St. Paul. Here there are bitter denunciation and blame for the Apostle's failure to comprehend that which he sought to teach:

> *Paul, Paul, I'd give*
> *My Greek inheritance, my wealth and youth*
> *To speak one evening with the Christ you love*
> *And never saw and cannot understand!*

Throughout the entire length of " Sappho in Levkas " there is a high lyrical nervous tension — a woman's confession of carnal sin — a sin which she has once enjoyed and which she enjoys again in the telling. It is a complete and detailed confession, but there is no repentance:

> *To think nobility like mine could be*
> *Flawed — shattered utterly — and by —*
> *This, this the shame, O Zeus, that Thou must hear —*
> *A slim, brown shepherd boy with windy eyes*
> *And spring upon his mouth!*

If one must have a label for Will's poetry, "lyrical in the classic tradition" would serve as well as another, perhaps. Still, not only did the imagined memories of the Golden Age of Greece, or the simple miracles of medieval times strike chords on his lyre; he also sings of the Mississippi River and the rich soil of the Delta and of the people who live upon it. In a sonnet to the River he captures its spirit:

> *Imperial indolence is thine and pleasure*
> *Of hot, long listlessness and moody course.*

On the death of a well-loved dog gone mad, he inspires not pity, not regret but the solacing hope of a friend in Eternity:

> *But as my prow scrapes on the marl,*
> *One watcher faithful, quaint,*
> *Will dash to meet me who am still*
> *His master, friend, and saint.*

Beginning in 1911, Will wrote poetry for twenty-five years. During this time he met and talked with world citizens. Athens, Paris, Italy, the South Seas were hosts to him. In between he managed to fight a war with his small furious body and burning mind. He was scared, he hated war — "It is the wickedest, most hateful thing man was ever guilty of" — yet he had to work like hell even to get in the Army: in the end he had to depend on the usual bananas and water to get by on weight. And when he came home he was a Captain, wearing a Croix de Guerre with a gold and a silver star. Feeling dead inside and incapable of emotion he was, nevertheless, able to write:

> *There never was a cause*
> *So worthy to be won!*

> *If France and England die,*
> *Freedom and faith are dead —*
> *Give them, O God, not heroes' hearts, but brains!*

During the twenty-five years of his creative work, he met with and talked to poets here and abroad. This was, it will be recalled, the era of revolt, the hoop-la era. Poets turned peddlers and proved more ingenious in advertising their wares than in perfecting their art. Groups and cults gathered in great numbers to quaff at the algae of public esteem like so many schools of minnows. Will Percy shunned all of these movements. He did not cry out in verse or before lecture audiences for an understanding of his genius. He made no struggle to liberate poetry from the older forms. Of his technique Will wrote:

"I tried to make it sound as beautiful and as fitting as I could. Old patterns helped, but if rhyme seemed out of place, the choruses of *Samson Agonistes*, some of Matthew Arnold's unrhymed cadences, and Shakespeare's later run-on pentameters suggested freer and less accepted modes of communication. As far as I can make out, the towering bulk of English poetry influenced me tremendously, but not any one poet, though I hope I learned as much as I think I owe to Browning's monologues and to Gilbert Murray's translations of Euripides."

He wrote a good deal and I find no evidence of any struggle either to conform or not to conform. He wrote gracefully, with ease, with beauty, with honesty and dignity. This seems to me important because it seems typical of the man as well as the poet.

Whether he was in Greece on the shores of the Aegean, or in Greenville on the banks of the Mississippi, Will Percy plucked his own lyre and sang his own songs to the stars and to the wind and to the dawn.

ROARK BRADFORD

PART I

SAPPHO IN LEVKAS, AND OTHER POEMS

SONG

O singing heart, think not of aught save song;
    Beauty can do no wrong.
  Let but th' inviolable music shake
    Golden on golden flake,
    Down to the human throng,
And one, one surely, will look up and hear and wake.

Weigh not the rapture; measure not nor sift
    God's dark, delirious gift;
  But deaf to immortality or gain,
    Give as the shining rain,
    Thy music pure and swift,
And here or there, sometime, somewhere, 'twill reach the grain.

SAPPHO IN LEVKAS

   Zeus, my Father, once again
I stand before Thee; once, and then no more.
   Here in the calm, deep night,
Far, far from Lesbos and the madness there,
  Here, where the alien sea about my feet
   Is clean and sacred with Thine awe,
   I come, Sappho, Thy child alone,
To speak with Thee as in the old, exalted days.
   In this last hour,
  Before the cool, regardless hand of death
   Erase me quite, desiring most to be
Most noble, I would break like nard before
Thy night-encurtained majesty my heart —
From hurt or shame withholding naught;
  Tell all, give thanks, and cease.
Nor would I have the flame of this, my prayer and baring,
  Shake with the breath of bitterness.
   Nor stay my heart, self-pitying,
   On that last human littleness,
Resentment 'gainst the gods.

     Thanks, Father, for
  The life that Thou hast given me.
  For it was high and full of joy — akin
  To those bright mountain spaces where
  A golden exaltation holds the peaks.
   Never, methinks, with more enamored hand

Hast Thou coaxed fire into the clay, than when
    In Lesbos, mine own mother grew with me.
    To Thee be thanks that in all life
'Twas mine to see goodness; that I, a woman,
    Beyond the tragic and the base of life,
Have seen to that serenity of right that flows
      Increasingly and always onward. Mine
Companions were that proved the race Thine offspring;
    Heroes and kings, sea-wanderers, poets, priests, —
      All, all, who, fervent, pass
      The flame of righteousness and truth
    To sequent generations yet asleep; and I
      Among them equal, praised and loved.
    More, Father; Thou hast given me the gift
      Of fragrant, fiery speech.
    Beyond the violet-circled isles, yea, to
      The confines of the habitable world
      My singing reached; nor can I think
    The time comes ever when the hearts of men
      So stripped of brightness be
But they will shake with rapture of my songs.
    Thou has made beauty mine own element,
      Taught me to drift, a burnished leaf,
    Down the long winds of ecstasy;
    And ever loveliness has swept my heart
      With lyric hand of rapture. Mine to feel
The majesty and tears and color of the sea;
      The awe and high obedience of the stars;
To watch at eve the saffron of Thy garment's hem;
      To wake unto Thy midnight messengers,
      The purple winds that roam infinity.

Yea, I, undoubtingly, have known
    The signs of immanent divinity
  In darkness, dawn, and dusk; and most,
    In music's passioning, when on the green,
      Beneath a frail, enchanted moon,
Some bard with mad, pale mouth sang urgently!

To think nobility like mine could be
  Flawed — shattered utterly — and by —
This, this the shame, O Zeus, that Thou must hear —
    A slim, brown shepherd boy with windy eyes
      And spring upon his mouth!
Mine Thou hast made the courage to face truth,
    Tho' truth were death; but face alone!
    Before Thine eyes to strip my passion till
Naked its evil gleams — here — now — oh, all
    The harsh and iron of my soul must forth
Ere shame's rebellion in my blood be quelled,
    And Thou familiar made with my reproach! . . .
Courage and truth, these two are not of earth!
Hearken Thou, Zeus, and judge if, at the last,
    In spite of all, I am not half divine,
      Loving these two.

    It was the hour of fleeing stars —
    If I should live to see a million dawns,
Each magic with a strange perfection of its own,
    The memory of none could stir as that
    The pool of tears and longing here within.
      The hour of fleeing stars —

And I, too, fled into the stillness,
Up from the quiet village to the hills
Where walk the morning-mooded gods.

A dawn of dew and hyacinths,
With grey-eyed, silver-footed April loose
Upon the hills. The arching air — the last few stars —
Each little leaf, tho' hushed, a-tremble to
The throbbing up of azure-hearted spring.
The upper meadows I had gained,
When on the eager silence came a sound,
A sleepy sound of many little feet.
Above the road I drew me up, and watched
The flock drift by. They passed, a huddled herd,
Shyly, and after them, with loitering foot
And bent, dark-curling head, the shepherd lad. —
Down, down, O heart of mine! — I feared to breathe
Lest breathing wake me from a dear enchantment;
I dared not move, lest moving stir the spell . . .
So leaned above the roadside — gazing —
Drinking the poison of his loveliness.
For he was lovelier than the youthful day;
More beautiful than silver, naked Ganymede!
Slowly he came beneath me on the road —
And suddenly I heard
The tremulous, soft magic give me speech.
" Shepherd, thy name! " He raised his head;
The wonder of his mouth and eyes and carven throat
Flooded me. And he smiled. So full
Of sweetness were those eyes, those curving lips,
A music as of tears swept through my veins;

And when his voice rose, answering,
　　As cool, unhurt, and clear it was
　　As is the bird-souled break of day.
" Phaon," he said, and, smiling still, passed on. —
　　Thus, Zeus, at dawn, seeking as was my wont,
　　　　The viewless god's companionship,
Phaon I met, himself in curve and color godlike,
　　And, meeting him, lost Thee!

When shining day aroused the earth and me,
I turned me from that roadside home, full-fledged
　　In Aphrodite. Not the gales of spring
Dashing the tenuous, frayed clouds high up the sky,
　　Were plumed with wilder rapture than my heart!
　　Nor was the earth's red longing for fruition
　　　　More hot than mine for Phaon . . .
　　Oh, I had loved the colors of the world,
　　All lofty things, all daring enterprise,
　　The glint and foam of life's adventuring!
　　That hour changed all the world and me!
　　　　Cool sleep became a haunted thing,
　　　　Full of the boy untruly amorous;
　　And waking, pain — a disillusionment
That filled the lonely day with thirst.
At dawn, at dusk, my feet sought out the hills
Beloved of shepherd folk, that, haply, sight of him
　　　　Might stay the burning here.
To glimpse his loveliness, to hear his voice
　　Answering lightly my light questionings
　　　　Was sweetness more than mortal thing,
More than the gods' ambrosial dalliance —

And bitterness, my heart, and bitterness!
  Oh, I grew studious in unlearning life,
    Till I could feign simplicity,
And use the simple speech of shepherd folk.
    My utmost intellect was bent to plan
      Assurance of chance meetings;
    My craft in beauty to devise which way
The yellow crocus in my hair might take his praise.
    At feasts and country festivals,
When came the dark and stars, I, too, came, there
    To see his bending body in the dance.
With not more grace, beneath the twilight breeze
Bending, the long-stemmed asphodel is swayed.
    But always something of his grace,
    His inextinguishable happiness,
Would seem to break my heart, and I would long to be
    Freed from that loneliness men call esteem,
    And there within the dance, a country wench,
Touching his shining arms, and breathing close
    His lithe and burning youth.

                O Thou hast known
The thousand years and each year's thousand lovers —
  What need to tell the pangs and tricks of clay
Common to all; yea, e'en at last to me, Thy child!
    Father, it seemed not evil then — so sweet
    He was; and I, who, most of all the world
      Loved purity and loathèd lust,
  Became the mark of mine own scorning ere
    I knew — he was so sweet!
A something from the freshness of the woods,

Of cool and shining leaves, of laggard winds,
    His beauty seemed to catch. I think
  The momentary blood that lights the rose
  Fired his veins with vintage of delight
    Perpetually. No lovelier
The first strong tulip, whose crimson arrogance
Lords it above blythe Eresos, and daunts
  The lesser darlings of pale April, than
    His mouth . . . And this, a shepherd boy!
His thoughts the thoughts of shepherds; his desires,
  The bread and water cravings of the poor.
  No trembling from the madness of my songs
Could reach his heart; no lofty converse call
    One cloud of questioning within
  His strange, unshadowed, listening eyes.
His lore was of the leaves, the clouds, the winds,
  What time the fields, a-frost with heliotrope,
    Yield richer pasturage; what time,
    The starrier meadows of wild broom.

This, this my lover! Mine, whose choice of mate
    Was bidden guest in all the courts
    And goodly palaces of Greece!
Lo, I, whose name was crowned thro' all the isles
    With praise and reverence,
  Grew stranger to the life that had been mine;
  Transmuted from the very certitude
  Of right example to reproach; become
As vacillant, weak flame before the wind of lust.
Yet, not, O Father, stained with deed of wantonness.
    I could not quite escape that holiness

       The sacred years had bred!
Methinks, the shepherd boy will never know
    But that one fragrant with a nobleness
He dimly felt, had found him for a space
       In some strange wise companionable.
    And at the last he loved me, Zeus! Oh, not
As lovers love — less than the shepherds' strife
    Of skill, less than the glowing dance,
Or merry gossip when the wine-vat teems.
       This irony for only anodyne
       Of all my pain Thou tenderest me —
    Out of the evil of my passioning came good!
       For Phaon, Phaon loved me as a goddess sent,
And, curbing grossness, looked to me for praise . . .
       Perhaps his blood was clean of lust,
    The mountains and the winds being pure,
    Or else his years, maturing loveliness,
       Left green that mortal taint.
     O soft, soft lies, beguile me not!
       Altho' by me unroused,
No doubt his manhood's proof will flaunt before
The red and white of some broad-bosomed wench
       Of his own kind — when I am gone!

     Oh, swiftly, swiftly, scorning shame,
Tell all, my heart, and make perpetual end . . .
    Thou send'st to mortals night as comforter;
And when the rounded moon breathes up the east,
Dost think to ease our most immedicable griefs
       With loveliness. But I am still
       Weary and broken with the memory

Of such a night, vouchsafèd lately.
Lesbos, my own, lay drowned beneath
The warm and argent flood of light — so still,
The very olive trees unstirring slept
A silver sleep. But, ah, to me the night
Was terrible with perfumes from the hair
And breasts of Aphrodite; within my blood,
Unstaunchable, surged all the undertow of spring,
Dragging my soul unto the sea that knows no law.
Haggard and parched, love's frenzy caught me up
And bore me from my dream-hot bed into the night.
My feet unconscious chose those pastures known
To love. The way was haunted with him; here
He stood; here leaned upon his crook to watch the dawn;
Here lifted up the wonder of his eyes.
And on the visioning leapt all the pity of
My life — vexing and hounding me.

About me, moonlight, stillness, empty night;
Distraught, I stumbled on.
A light, near footstep sounded suddenly;
I lifted filmy eyes; saw; reeled; and saw
Again — Phaon, the shepherd. Then madness broke.
His argent throat and arms,
His mouth, the dew, the tenderness — O God! —
I bent me to him with the flaming cry,
" Phaon — I love thee; one kiss, one kiss — Phaon! "
A silence came. The night grew huge and cold.
Silence. I lifted heavily,
A nightmare weight, my lids and looked upon the boy.
Amazement held him, wonder; quick

His eyes avoided mine, then, dubious, sought;
   And in the miserable stillness there,
   I watched the radiance leave his face,
  And pain steal up like age. Within me died
All fire. I closed my eyes; the night whirled past.
     Anguish like bolted lightning showed
  In that long instant what myself had been to him —
   One alien to the lowness of his life;
   Almost a holy thing, a-stir with God,
That now revealèd stood of common grossness.
   As dreadful as their lovelessness,
The scorning that I knew his eyes would show!
Tho' never loved, yet never to be loathed —
That mean respect at least my pride might save!
   I woke, beheld the desperate urgency,
   And faced him with a lie that heaven sent.
" O shepherd, I leave Lesbos, home, and thee
At dawn. Good-bye." Then hid from him my face,
   And bowed before the surge of agony.
I needed not to see his joyous tenderness
    Pulse back; I knew, how bitterly!
Before him, broken, cold, and blind, I felt
  Him take me in his arms, all gentleness,
And on my mouth lay his, a long, long kiss.
  The music of his voice was far away;
" Come soon again to Lesbos and the shepherds here
   Who love thee " . . .

        Thus,
  As I had prayed, I lay upon his breast,
  And in his cloudy glamour was wrapped close,

And breathed the fragrance of his neck and hair —
   Yet not as I had prayed. Midmost
  The snatch of starved, impossible delight —
His lips to mine — the reeling moonlight — passion —
   I knew the irony, the tragic mockery.
    While yet I clung to him, he seemed
Almost a child, sweet as a child is sweet,
      Unsparingly; and I —
Old — in the world and sin and vision, old;
   He but a shepherd boy; and I — Sappho!
   So when he had released me from his arms,
    Stricken and blind, with one swift kiss
Upon his brow, one sobbed " Good-bye," I turned;
   So, fleeing, down into the darkness.

    Unto perfection I was born;
 The shepherd boy, who would not see my sin,
    Recalled me to myself. That was the end . . .
     Imperative to keep my soul superb,
     For his sake, mine, and Thine,
      And one sole method to that end.
    But lest my resolution should be wax
 Beneath his nearness, and because I chose
     To speak with Thee apart, in calm,
   I minded me of those, my lying words.
Therefore, when morning bore the harbor ships
     Upon their devious, blue wanderings,
 Myself, beneath a glistening sail, wide-eyed,
    Gazed on the fading island that I loved,
       A last, long time on Lesbos . . .

Think not, O Zeus, I render me to death
   Because the shepherd loved me not.
   Such pain as many mortals bear,
   Myself would scorn to shun.
  Sterner than unrequited love the cause,
      And not unpitiful. . . . Perhaps in time
My burnt, high-bosomed beauty might have lured
   His blood — No, no! not that! not possible!
Hearken, O God, the truth, the utter truth!
   Had mine been siren sorcery
   To draw him tremulous to my desire,
   And had he answered love with love,
   Passion with passion, ardent equally —
I know that I had cooled — the wanton's trick —
Found tedious what had been bliss, grown strange,
   At last, despised! More — more — I stifle —
      If far from Lesbos and from him
   I should remain — I should forget the boy!
And this — indignant heart of mine, I will not lie —
   Could Phaon's magic pass,
   Yet other snares, perhaps as sweet — if such
   Could be, — would trap and madden me as his.
   Some summer-tinted mouth, some curvèd throat;
   The Bacchic grace of some young body, bare
And glistening in the games — I know . . . I know . . .
Perhaps some throbbing, lawless-eyed barbarian,
   Sea-burnt, gorgeous, and bestial —
      Surely, not that, my God!
      But always I shall be
Hurt with the vehemence of too, too perfect beauty;

    Bare and resistless always
  To all the sorceries of fair, fair flesh! . . .

    Enough . . . The truth hath sickened me . . .
    But all is told, and now comes rest.
I would make calm my brow and heart for death.
One step across this darkling cliff, and in
  The ocean's weary breathing I am caught,
Made one, assuaged forever. Yet I pause . . .
  The bitter sea with its pale tentacles
  Of foam half seen below my feet cannot
    Now make me truckle unto cowardice,
Who knew not fear in life . . . But is it life,
Not death, I dare not face? 'Tis surely ill
    The wine of life to spill contemptuously,
    Wearied, in wantonness, or in despite.
If, though, the wine of its own nature sour,
    Lose all the jewel and the perfume, shall
The drinker pause to cast it back to earth?
      Why spare the rose
  Doomed to the worm? The soul incurably
    Hurt with a crescent sin? T' avoid
  The loosened shaft of seen necessity
    Is wisdom, not some trick of fear.

To me, my kinship with immortal things
  Hath been too clear revealed that I should watch
    With willingness my retrogression to the clay
    And baseness mortals own as parent.
Either the starry, wind-swept, sea-enraptured soul

Of me, myself, myself shall last unto the end.
   Or summonable death shall quench me out
      Undimmed, exalted still.
   No cowardice, O Zeus, I swear!
   With all my spirit I have ever fought
   Life's battles; nor testing conflict shunned,
When righteousness made part. But when the enemy
   Thou sett'st against me is the sacred element,
      The prime nobility that wings my spirit,
What boots the battle? And the event — defeat
      Or victory alike — is utter ruin.
To me hath beauty been the ripple and the light
      That proved a sea divine,
Sweeping the stars, our little universe, all, all,
Into the wave of some sublime and glittering doom.
      Oh, always beauty was to me
         Thyself half seen, my Father.
   In windy leaves and grass, thy laughter loose,
   In yellow noon, thy nectared, slumberous ease,
Thy clean and lofty joy in high, sun-striken woods,
      In storms thy restlessness, thyself
         In this vast, darkling sea.
   And this same beauty now betrayeth me.
   So long as life by it is made divine,
   So long by it am I made harlot-hearted.
      No cure, no cure! but oh,
That such perfection in such wise should be
      Rifted, and out of harmony!
Methinks, Thyself, the author of the flaw,
Must doubt Thy fathering wisdom.
Indeed, indeed, beneath their calm content,

Thou and the other gods must feel the tears
    That make the human breast almost divine,
      To see me thus, alone and lonely,
    That once was Sappho, song o' the world. . . .
    And yet no wind of heaven beareth me
Breath of compassioning. . . . Perhaps they laugh or scorn.
    Oh, can it be that in the halls of heaven
The very gods are tainted with the Cyprian's sin?
What if the bestial gossip told of them be true,
    And too authentic be the lecherous tales
        Of Io and the rest?

    Then will I break with all the gods,
And more divine than they, snuff out this flame
    Ere it be vile with universal degradation!
O night, O night, am I the only struggling thing?
    Doth any cry save mine rise to thy stars
Against the tyranny of flesh and mortal grossness?
      O mothering darkness, fold
      Obliteration closer round me, for
    Mine eyes blur, and my throat is hurt
        With welling pain. . . . Tears, tears,
Ye rob me of the little left me, godly pride,
        And leave me woman. . . .
    And I had thought the hour that summed
    And closed my lonely struggle for perfection,
    Had been a thing of triumph. It is pitiful.
Leaning across this sea here in the night,
    A moment's space from death, I can recall
No old, high legend whereupon to lean my heart.
Instead, I seem to know the rain-grey, hungering eyes

Calypso bent across the surge that gave
    And took forever her delight.

The deep air, too, seems somehow cleansed with tears,
    And cooler grown. The stars are not so close.
    A breath of silver up the sky! Again —
        Dawn! dawn! O Zeus,
      The dawn that I had thought to never see!
      Eastward the cold light brims into the sky
And joyous sweeps away the stars that watched with me.
They come no more. . . . Dawn. . . . Dawn, and spring
        again!
      This grey and lucent hour, light sleep
    Steals from the shepherds' clustered curls,
    And leaves them dewy as the bended grass.
    At home it is a dawn of dew and hyacinths,
With silver-footed April loose upon the hills.
      Along the curving road the flocks
    Lag half asleep, lag, but still come
        Nearer and nearer till —
Oh, the insufferable beauty of his bending head!
        O home! O Lesbos!
      To lean above that roadside, breathless,
      And see again the shepherd boy I love —
        His thonged and sandalled grace —
        His bare, brown throat —
      The violets careless round his head —
    Those eyes of spring and unawakened fire —
The dew and roses of the mouth that once I kissed!
Forget, forget all else, O gods, and grant this boon!
    Bear me back home to Lesbos and the boy!

Steep me but one short hour in his love!
　　Oh, let the anguished crimson of his mouth
Seek fire from mine, and all his brown, light grace
Flame into strength to crush my paleness; let
　　His morning eyes know drought and noon,
The haze of hidden tears, the film of hope,
　　And me the only cool and dew.
One misty, scarlet kiss within your arms —
　　　　Phaon! Phaon!
I would forswear song — beauty — Zeus, my father . . .

Ah, — madness — madness — uncoil, old anguish! . . . Ah!
　　O cool, grey wind of dawn! O sea! —
　　Thou harlot-hearted woman, sleep!
And wake thou, Sappho, leafy-templed child of God!
　　Upon the lovely world another day. . . .
　　Come, fearless, piteous heart of mine . . . come. . . .
At last the comfort and the cleansing of the sea.

CHORUS

(AFTER THE GREEK)

Surely in no benignant mood
The gods have fashioned us, but craftily
　　To send us homing to the sod
Wise only in our own futility.

　　With hyancinthine brows of youth,
We enter life as to a festival;
　　But, ere the feast is spread, the gods
Snatch back the wine, the song, the coronal.

　　And, lusterless, we turn, afraid,
Turn to the sole vouchsafèd heritage,
　　And in the shaken darkness clutch
The disenchanted ledges of old age.

TO A MOCKING-BIRD

Thy taunting happiness,
Thy overbold upflashing bliss,
Pierces my heart to-night, O mocking-bird!
Beneath the limpid surge of darkness,
The awe of stars and all the hush,
Thou flingest far thy little joy, unawed —
Flushed with some momentary triumph,
Or stray, delicious whim.
The tumult of thy silver mockery
Shakes through the trees, across the trancèd lawn,
And rouses weariness to pain within my heart.
Cease, cease thy rapture!
To-night the courage and the joy are gone;
I would forget the battles and the ceaseless clash,
The long, rewardless surge of strife,
The race run and no laurels,
The fight fought and no guerdon.
To-night, only to-night, 'tis sweet
No more to buffet with the winds of grief
But bend to them, luxuriously abandoned.
Again the light notes leap
In gusts of gaiety!
Ah, bird, thy song, derisive of defeat
And age and the inevitable doom,
Is but the song of mine own people —
The conquerors, the unafraid —
And thou, in thy bright arrogance and fearless bliss

Summest the spirit of a newer age,
    The unprophetic confidence
Of this new-sinewed western world.

Cease, cease thy song of triumph and unwisdom!
To-night I long to hear an alien sweetness that
        Long vision hath made sad.
    Oh, for a silver-steepèd garden overseas,
        Hung with too poignant perfumes,
Where thy frail sister lifts her piteous cry,
        Her little hidden cry,
    Sharp with a hundred centuries of pain,
        Hurt with the constant woe,
    The weariness and all the tears
    Of generations that have gone, darkly!
    Oh, to forget this western flaunt of living!
        To breathe in those far lands that air
Breathèd by dreamers dead, lovely and purposeless;
To hear the anguished nightingale that Sappho heard;
    To see beneath the moon the olive trees
        And cypresses asleep, as when Antinous,
    With eastern-scented brows and poppy lids
        Looked forth, godlike, upon them;
    To catch, perhaps, — the myrtle boughs between —
        Glimpse of that unforgettable, sweet sea
    That heard of yore Sicilian shepherd boys
        Piping across their shining pastures,
        That still, upon the shores of Ithaca,
Beareth the blue, Homeric, star-entangled tide!

ALL SOULS' DAY

    Quiet with amber light
The pale enfolding afternoon;
    In sleep the slow leaves fall;
Tranquil as misting tears or swoon,
    The pendent blue that bears
No cloud except the daylight moon.

    Opal, a-drowse, and vast,
The river takes its southward way;
    And southwards sweep the birds,
Swift and mysterious and grey. . . .
    Do so the gusty dead
Wing the warm air in troops to-day?

    Surely this peacefulness
Of feathered fields of golden-rod,
    The wistful, songless trees,
And asters clouding from the sod,
    Them, homing, lure from out
The bleak infinitudes of God.

    Oh, surely all the south
Our prayers and dear remembrance make
    Calls from the cold, blue tides
Their wings to-day, and they forsake
    Their solemn ways for us,
Remembering death and all the ache.

And thou, so lately one —
Not all the new adventuring
    In starry realms can hold
Thee from return. To-day thy wing,
    Pausing above my heart,
Doth courage and assurance bring.

A PAGE'S ROAD SONG

(13TH CENTURY)

Jesu,
If Thou wilt make
Thy peach trees bloom for me,
And fringe my bridle path both sides
With tulips, red and free,
If Thou wilt make Thy skies as blue
As ours in Sicily,
And wake the little leaves that sleep
On every bending tree —
I promise not to vexen Thee
That Thou shouldst make eternally
Heaven my home;
But right contentedly,
A singing page I'll be
Here, in Thy springtime,
Jesu.

SOARING

My heart is a bird to-night
That streams on the washed, icy air.
My heart is a bird to-night
'Twixt the stars and the branches bare.

My heart is abroad to-night
Rushed on by the fierce, crystal air.
No nest will it seek to-night
In the branches, ice-brittle and bare.

Wide-wingèd my heart to-night
With joy on the surge of the air.
What matter that spirits of night
Make shudder the trees, lean and bare!

FOR MUSIC

O singer, canst thou summon up
    The early blue-bird's wing?
The pang of those uncertain days
    That swoon with unborn spring?

O singer, canst thou summon up
    The crimson of the rose,
The silver gloom of April dawns,
    The breathless unrepose;

The yearning in the dark divine,
    Deep woods, a-bloom and dumb,
The starry, tear-blurred nights of May
    That bring delirium?

O singer, canst thou summon up
    In music all the spring
Whose crowding incense caught my heart
    So long ago? — Then sing!

AUTUMN TUNE

Sweeter than spring, sweeter than spring,
These brown and blue and lingering
      Soft days that wing
Like filmy dreams across the world,
One by one unfurled, unfurled,
Where the ripe fields slumber and glitter and swing.

Sadder than song, sadder than song,
The choral drowse with madness strong
      That all day long
The locusts lift to their god the sun,
For joy of the life that is almost done —
Raptured and shrill and regretless throng.

Wilder than wings, wilder than wings,
The flight of the golden leaves when springs
      The fear that flings
Them swirling and shining up from the bare
Dark branches that reach to the calm of the air
Where death is a-dream on azure wings.

A SEA-BIRD

I cry, I cry
Into the night.
Along the waves
I gleam and fly
A haunted flight;
A cry, a cry
Into the night.

Lone, alone,
And the sea is mad.
Mourning, mourning,
Broken and strown,
It nurseth the dead,
The dead alone —
And my heart that is mad.

ECSTASY

(AFTER VERLAINE)

The moon shines now
White in the woods;
From every bough
Cometh in floods
A voice divine . . .
O love of mine!

The pool of jet,
Deep mirror sees
In silhouette
The willow trees
That moan and gleam . . .
O hour of dream!

Tender and vast,
A peacefulness
Drifts downward past
The shadowless
Star-purple night . . .
Hour of delight!

IN AN AUTUMN WOOD

Thou, too, O bronze-eyed darling of the feast,
Under the deep, brown leaves and faded sky
      At last wilt lie,
Forgetful of the joy thy beauty leased.

But ere that time, how many times, alas,
Wilt thou with careless hand sweep all the vain,
      Taut strings of pain
That are my heart nor hear the hurt chords pass.

Almost I wish to-day that thou didst lie
Beyond the leaves, unsummonably still —
      So well, so ill
I love thy loveliness that hears no cry.

PRISON SONG

Beat, beat, wings of my heart,
Stormy and swift as you will!
Beat and break, but the walls of the world
Will hold you captive still.

Oh, the bird of the moon flies into the west
To dip in the sun's lagoon,
And, following her, the wild geese blur
In the depths of a golden swoon.

But, heart of mine, O bird of my heart,
Tho' they curve to the sunken stars,
You follow not with the strain of your wings,
For between — the iron bars.

THE RETURN OF THE LEAVES

Leaves and the sweet-choired blue;
And my heart set free again.
Leaves, leaves and the dew;
Free, but not free from pain.

The laughter of June is shed;
And my heart gives heed again.
But, ah, for youth that is fled,
Fled, with all but its pain.

MARCH MAGIC

Once more the fickle birds return
    Across the sloping seas,
And strew the tender fields again
    With their old melodies.

The sky is magic as the month,
    Low sun, high stars between,
The icy winds have washed it clear;
    But it, too, dreams of green.

The boats are breathing on the sea;
    They cannot wait for men;
Some undertide has brought them word
    Straight from a blue-starred fen.

Unpiloted they steal away,
    No man shall see them soon,
The sea birds follow but a mile,
    Then leave them to the moon.

We, too, shall steal upon the spring
    With amber sails blown wide;
Shall drop, some day, behind the moon,
    Borne on a star-blue tide.

Enchanted ports we, too, shall touch,
    Cadiz or Cameroon;
Nor other pilot need besides
    A magic wisp of moon.

ST. FRANCIS TO THE BIRDS

    Daytime? The stars quite gone?
O brother Sleep, you tripped me in my prayers,
And bound me in your scarves of colored dreams!
      Pray God the brethren find me not
      Flat in the dew and just awake.
      Fie! fie! thou slug-a-bed!
Up! kneel to thine orisons — compose thy robe —
   And get thee from this green and idle wood
      Back to the world!
   Alas, the summer air hath blown
Shame from my heart! Jesu, the prayers must wait —
    Light-hearted day on naked feet
Runs thro' the woods, and I must watch her here
    Shaking the boughs above my head,
And winning with her rogueries the leaves' applause.
      Delicious so! . . .
   Idler, pagan, Francis, up! Ah, well —

     Prophets and patriarchs!
     What company is this?
     The blessed birds of God —
    Silent and orderly, row on row,
Thick on the branches, scholarwise on the grass —
Sparrows and swallows, bobolinks and larks —
Tiny and big, and gay- and hempen-gowned —
   Attentive all and silent; eyes on me —
   Littlest children, my brothers — O birds,

Good morrow! For your presence thanks. . . .
    And yet, may I confess —
Beseeching you will not mistake my ignorance
For lack of gentleness or knightly courtesy —
I know not quite what mission draws you here?
Only has Father Noah seen such multitudes.
Is it, perchance, with tree-top news you come
    Requiring such deliverance?
    Alack, I have not any roof at all,
    Much less an ark.
But should your needs petition one, content yourselves;
    The brethren shall be willing carpenters.
Your watchful eyes and silence, courteous and prim,
    Betray I have mistook your coming's cause.
    Perhaps on your first-waking flights,
    Beholding me so quiet in the grass,
You thought me dead, and came with friendly haste
    To hide in leaves my obvious corruption.
    Three hops and a silver chuckle —
Robin, irreverent robin, wrong again?
Ho! ho! at last the dear God sends me sense!
    A sermon 'tis! Robin, I guessed!
    Come nearer, darling children, close!
O lovely cloud of wings! O tiny storm of twitter!
    What barren faith was ours
    To pass you by these many days
Without one salutation in Christ's name,
Or news of His impending kingdom once!
Let these poor words win your forgiveness,
And His, whose frailest ones we have o'erlooked.

Brethren! . . .
        Ahem! —
                (Saints! what text can serve!)
" In those days Jesus said:
My Father's kingdom may be likened to
    A grain of mustard seed,
Which, being sown, is smallest of all seeds,
But, growing up, is greatest of all herbs,
Till in the shadow of its branches lodge
    The birds of heaven."
    Yet, no! these words He never spoke.
    He knew as you or I
The idle ways of summer, and the fields
Where poppies in their silken kerchiefs crowd the wheat,
And, when the dry, quick autumn winds had stripped
    their scarlet,
He, too, had seen their tiny million seeds —
Mere dust beside the mustard's burliness.
    Mark nodded or forgot, poor fisherman!
    How often thus they understood Him not!
And in these far-off days their surface words we seize,
    Set up, adore, and miss the gospel underneath
        Forgetting they were simple men,
And He, dear God, who only aimed at simpleness.
But still He did say Heaven's kingdom was a tree,
A mighty tree with branches' room for all,
And sunny babblement of leaves where all
His wingèd ones might skim and shine at ease.
    O little, brown minores,
Come — let's skip the text! But after it

In any well-conducted sermon comes, you know,
The exhortation. Now I should proclaim
The evil of your lives and urge repentance!
When summer dawn is here? and only choristers?
       How may it be?
   What evils may I warn your hearts against?
       What words of guidance give?
     None come to me. . . . No ownership is yours,
But winds and trees and evening waters and the sun
   Are yours in largesse, without counterclaim —
The eighth commandment was not meant for you!
I would not coax you from your ways of lechery;
     For not your will, but God's,
Fills all the April air with mating and the chirp
   Of love. Obedient be to His good season.
      I think ye do no murder, yet —
   Sometimes it grieves my very soul to see
The lesser brethren fly your swift pursuit.
If God directed so you take your livelihood,
'Tis well, but spare, I pray, their tiny span of bliss
   If food less petulent may serve instead;
   Nor their destruction ever make your sport.
     Little children, no rebuke is meant;
      I only pray your gentleness. . . .
     Indeed, indeed, He set your flight
   Above the paths of sin! Advise? conjure?
     I do you wrong. Rather, I think,
He put it in your hearts to come to me
      Not judging I could give
   Morsel of help or little twig of truth,
But that the comfort of your presence might be mine.

For sometimes, little brethren of the woods,
We, in the common world beneath your trees,
So clearly see the weakness and the sin about,
   That only them we see, and we forget
The holiness that still persists, the light, yea, God, Himself!
   Belike He feared for me such hour,
And in His care sent you, His seraphs of the trees.
For you, tho' of the world, share not its taint,
   Nor breathe nor know its sin.
If we lived so, the sudden curve
   And anxious fanning of soft plumes
      Would stir our bending heads,
And off we'd fly to — to that same mustard tree of yours!

      Was ever such a sermon?
         I, no text; no morals, you!
   Let's call it then no sermon, but instead
I'll sit within the shadow of this tree
      With you companionably close,
And while the hoyden breeze on emerald wings
Lets through the shimmering lances of the sun,
And hums aloud for wantonness — we'll gossip!
      Oh, not of sin or other grave concern,
But right familiarly of what we know — His life.
         Saints! what a fluttering
         And sparkle of expectancy!
      Upon my lap at last, robin of mine?
         'Twas thus about His knees that day
         The children came and begged for tales,
         Vexing poor Matthew, and bequeathing us
         His dearest page.

Let me see . . . ah . . .
The book is not so full of tales for birds;
'Twas writ for men, you see.
I doubt not men had far the greater need —
'Twas not because he loved you less!
But now I do recall a story; one you'll love —
That day by Jordan!
They had been urchin comrades years before,
That lonely Jordan prophet and our Lord,
But him the wilderness and stars and solitude
Had swallowed up this many a day.
So now his eyes were full of tears
To see, across the grass where all the people sat,
The little boy he loved run to him, call his name,
And in the cool, clear water kneel
To beg his blessing.
The desert had not dried his heart away;
And so he wept, and clasped Him close, and prayed. . . .
But I'd forgot the Holy Ghost!
He could have been
A scarlet cloud of seraphim, a lightning bolt,
Fire or darkness, what He willed!
But what chose He? what creature honored there?
From out of Heaven He flew — a lovely dove!
That was a day for birds!
Sure, you must love the Holy Ghost — and keep
Your hearts and plumage clean and bright for Him,
And make your mourning baths baptismal in a way!
Another story I recall, dear children.
But whether it be writ or only dreamed
I cannot say. . . . Gethsemane . . .

My heart is there so much, I do remember more,
Perhaps, than they that set it down. . . .
It is not spring talk for a golden dawn,
But even you, gleamers of God, should know.
Before the end He longed to come once more
To that familiar garden that He loved.
Its olive trees and sandy barrenness
That drank the moon were home to Him,
For other home He had not, save
Such waste and lonely places off the way
As men forgot. And so that night, the last, He knew,
That He might pray together with the twelve,
He came unto the garden where it lay
All full of moonlight and of silence,
And with Him brought for comfort them He loved.
Indeed, He loved us all — too well, too well —
But ah, the mortal of His heart had need to choose
For special tenderness, those few.
How tired He was! Oh, weary unto death;
And needed most mere human love!
But they whom He had chosen, whom He loved,
His own, His very own — they slept!
God! God!
Had Lancelot or Tristran been His knights,
They had not slept. . . .
When those we love have failed us in our need
There is no bitterness undrunk for death. . . .
That night, as thus He lay,
After the prayer, too tired for tears,
And even God forgot Him with the rest,
I think that one of you, beholding from

The shadows where you hid, that agony,
Trembled and paused and bent your head,
Then, for you knew no other, quavered forth
Your silver serenade for healing to His heart. . . .
The torches and the sudden faces broke
Your song. . . . Likely He never heard . . .
But only you bethought to comfort Him that night. . . .

They slept . . . God! Let me back into the world!
    Lest coming suddenly again
    He finds them sleeping still.
      Good-bye, good-bye!
Remember to give thanks each day to Him
Who made your feathers clean and fair and warm,
Who set within your hearts clear springs of happiness,
Who shares with you His home, the sacred sky.
And I beseech you, little brothers, think
On us, who, soaring, never leave the earth.
O swallows, should you see, when evening comes,
One leaning from his darkened window, dark,
His eyes unlighted, bitter with the day's defeat,
Toss where your vagrant flight may catch his gaze;
For, as you scatter up the golden sky,
Haply he may remember Jacob's dream,
The ladder and the wings, and, holpen, send his **heart**
In God's light careless way to climb with you.

    And you, sweet singers of the dark,
That tune your serenades but by the stars,
      Love gardens most;
For garden casements do unlock themselves
With magic silentness unto your spell,

And music unto sleepless eyes doth bring
The lonely solace of unloosened tears.
But most, you morning choristers, that haunt the eaves,
Whose little voices like a hundred stars
Shine just before the sun, tapping with dreams
The lazy sleep that lingers on our lids,
Fail not to keep your matins clear for us;
And should you know, by some bird craft of yours,
The room wherein an almost mother lies,
Choir your sweetest there, as tho' the babe to come
Were son of God — for so he is!
Again, farewell!

    I cannot leave ye thus!
     O Father, I have failed!
     What truth can they recall
      That I have given them?
   None, none! And now the hour is past!
Birds, birds, stay yet and harken this last word,
Too simple to be long remembered; but, forgot,
Taking the shining and the wings
And all seraphic meaning from the life we know —
And you that glisten through the lovely blue,
Not singly, but in shoals and multitudes,
Bear witness to the truth that I would tell:
That child of God, man-child or bird-child
Or silver-wingèd star-child of the night,
That lives apart, unto himself,
Unsharing, unsolicitous, and free,
Hath vainly lived; for life, this present life,
Is but the throe to brotherhood!

Behold our hearts, which we forget to hide,
Are fashioned so in likeness to His own,
That only joy of all can bring them bliss,
And every special woe must bring them pain.
So long as one,
But one of all His children knoweth grief,
So long we sorrow too. Nor can there be a heaven
Till hell be tenantless. . . .
The love we bear hath neither gates nor walls
To keep men out, but tendereth itself
A refuge city to the shelterless,
Calling across the tempest-shadowed plain
Unceasingly, " Come in, come in! "
And, for they will not come, but scatter far,
Grieving and hurt and blind into the storm,
There is no peace for us, and all our days
Are hungered for the sight of them that stray,
Are empty to the cry that sounds in vain,
" Come in, come in! " . . .

      So must it be — now.
But I perceive another day not too far off;
And in that day there shall not one remain
Uncleansed of tears and sin and every stain;
And in that day, behold, the golden droves
Of His light creatures shall invade the dawn,
Shall stream across the hush beyond all stars,
And people those celestial places He hath planned.

    Some day. . . . But now . . .
I go to them that have the greater need.

God's blessing steep your hearts in peace,
And all your deeds in patient tenderness.

My name! . . . They call me through the woods!
Quick, quick! away! . . . Here, Egidio! I come!
Up, up into the leaves lest seeing you
They say there was a miracle!
Go! But birds, my birds, come back to me!

ARCADY LOST

The cherry bloom and robin time of year
Again is come; and we that shepherd still
Among less heavenly pastures feel the fear
Of spring again, and all the tears that thrill
But never fall. Last night, across the shine
Of iris-tinted skies, I heard the dim
Enraptured song we knew, the dire divine
Music, that once, beyond the violet rim
Of pain, could waft us clear to where, our own,
Th' unstable faery shores of ecstasy
Burn in the twilight of an April sea.
Our music came last night to me alone.

No more may song nor petalled fluttering
Upbreathe frail, frail delight as in the days
We clung together here. Instead, they bring
The pain of hearts that, glamourous still with spring,
Break, and the dread of star-lit, lonely ways
Where once, O comrade mine, we heard them sing.

ON LEAVING TAORMINA

O almond trees, beneath whose fruited shade
I lay these summer days and saw the sea,
The hills of Mola, and Calabria's jade,
Good-bye! Perhaps the god that yielded me
Such luxury of happiness, these clear
And brimming hours with you, will, in his grace,
Yield none again; and, summer, finding here
Your branches green, will find again the place
I love, not me. Thro' all the leafy years,
Others will come and love your loveliness;
Love with a heart as gay and free of fears
As mine, and, leaving, leave their souls no less.
But, ah, for me, when spring stands in the door,
Take on, I pray, one shade of pink the more.

DUSK: ASSUAN

Serene, he mounts the minaret of day;
Where purple spreads the world his footsteps pause.
Splendors from whence he rose still flame his grey
And amethystine robes to golden gauze.
Priestly and pure, he stands within the curve
Precipitous that fronts the chasmed west.
The blowing birds that wove his hem in swerve
And arabesque of jet, flicker to rest.
And now his voice, a tide of silence, pours
Across the desert's pallor and the palms:
" Come forth to God from all your darkened doors."
Who pause for prayer? Partake the sacred calms?
Pass and repass the women with their jars;
But faithful come those worshipers, the stars.

THE COAST OF BOHEMIA

Like some still angel who, in toilless might,
The empyrean cleaves with unstirred wings,
Heedless of his proud speed save where it springs
About his feet like blown, quick-curling light —
So passed our ship in soft, gloom-charmèd flight,
Midmost a huge, drear shade of sea and air,
Voiceless, indissoluble, saving where
Prowwards awoke two folds of fiery white.
The wash of dim infinity, the swoon
Of vasty quiet hushed us. Then the least
Dawn quivered — nay, the east dreamed of the moon.
Breathless, we watched. Again! Ah, elfin east!
The white day leaped upon the world. The miles
Of sea flamed loose — and then we saw those isles.

TO THE MISSISSIPPI

They came from fierce, burnt Spain to seek for gold
Upon thy shores, and with superb, strange prows
Dazzled the wilderness. Their proud, swarth brows
With gorgeous lust of gems and trove made bold
The river folk feared as the gods of old.
But, lo! thy gods awaking, the deep drowse
Of death their chief assuaged of quests and vows,
And him, not disillusioned, thou didst fold.
No dreams of gold or jeweled glebe now force
Thy stream with ships adventuring; and tho'
Thy flood in yellowed opulence doth flow,
'Tis not from stain of deep, corroded treasure.
Imperial indolence is thine and pleasure
Of hot, long listlessness and moody course.

IN DALMATIA

A brotherhood of bleached, air-scourgèd peaks
In desolation watch the Illyrian sea.
Them twice the lidless day brings ecstasy;
Their leperous fronts but twice a splendor freaks.
Once, when the anguish-heedful dawn unspeaks
Their woe with rich, deep-blushed divinity;
Again, when 'neath eve's balm they tower free
Like Tyrian tents of purple-amorous sheiks.
As they with light, so man with vision twice
Scorns pain. First, when the bowl of life in bliss
Youth holds, sees all — grape, dregs, and sleepy spice —
Then stoops his head to drink as tho' to kiss.
And last, when to the verge of death he strives,
Pauses to gaze adown, and, smiling, dives.

INVOCATION

Sleep of the coolèd lids and breath of flowers,
O sleep of youth, dew-sandaled from the leas,
Throated with music of ensilvered showers
And silken winds that flash against the trees;
O summer sleep of passionate innocence,
Clean as the morning stars of doubt and pain,
If dreamful, not, oh, not at the expense
Of tears, but fresh with news from fancy's Spain —
Revisit with thy trancèd healing sweet
These eyes that have forgot almost thy spell,
Sail back with all thy joyous-freighted fleet
Down the long azure of my spirit's swell.
And for thy traffic with that brooding stream
Bring back the purple to my hills of dream.

TO CHATTERTON

Immortal boy! whose years scarce reached my own,
And yet were filled with all the kinless grief
Devolving on old age, without relief
Of stagnant brain, of nerveless blood and bone —
At dusk, when wind-swept autumn woods are lone,
I, who of Fortune's bounty am the thief,
Gold-filled, I muse upon thy life, so brief,
So passionate, and, envying thee, I moan.
For dreaming thus, there comes a specter thought
Which fastens on my soul and leaves it grey
With fear. If Death, who found thy field so fraught
With golden harvest, now to me should say
" Enough, 'tis Autumn " — God! no harvest yet
Have I, and still my fields are green and wet.

THE SILENT SINGERS

And Proserpine, still fragrant of the air
And upper brightness, bore him children — him
Whose heart, not knowing Sicily, was bare
Of songs, whose sunless mouth was dumb. That grim
Illimitable cold was alien
Always; and always, hopeful of the song
Of birds, she leaned and thought to find again
Those blooms that watch the tearless stars so long
They weep. When to her kingdom came the dead,
Still glistening with tears and asphodel,
Forgetting all save home, their eyes she read,
Wherein the sweet, far earth seemed yet to dwell.

. . . . .

Behold, the blue South in our hearts like wine —
But Pluto's mouth, O Mother Proserpine!

WILD GEESE

When naked winter on the midnight falls
With icy macerations, hook and flail,
They come — with rush of wings and signal calls —
The mighty birds that home the north, full sail
Upon the blast. Their unseen cohorts high,
Breasting the stars, make purpose proud to shun
All pausing, till beneath them, tranquil, lie
Day and the silver marshes of the sun.
But should the floor of darkness festal grow,
As far beneath some town unbraids its lights,
Routed, deceived, heart-set to gain the glow,
They drop; nor join again the sunward flights.

Was it their cries I heard, remote, withdrawn,
Or spirit choirs dark-flying towards some dawn?

FAILURE

For them that on the mountain fight beneath
The visioned ensigns of the unknown God,
Tho' battle-anguish be their only wreath,
Failure their palm, their victory the sod —
I have no tears. Compassion not that band,
Patriots, poets, dreamers, men of prayer,
The common reachers after right. The hand
Impelling them thus blindly to lay bare
Their hearts to that unequal contest, grants
Solace divine for their divine attempt.
For them that know not strife, nor hear the chants
Precedent to the bloody end's contempt —
For them unloose your tears! Their life is sleep,
Unvigilant, unwounded; they but sheep!

EX ÆTATE

Not for more hours of bliss I make demand,
O life! So many thou hast flung with hand
Of summer. Grant instead for winter's hem
Of sunshine, certain memory of them.

TO MILTON

As well house up the homeless Bedouin stars
And tent them permanent on the night's great desert,
As thy steep thoughts to circumscribe and fix
With human tears or home or human love; —
Thou nomad of God's universal night!

TO LUCREZIA

Pause we within the sunset, love;
Rare is such time — so lovely and so passionless —
And sweeter far than when the proud, gold morning
Withers the dew with scorn and in his youth.
    Pause here and let me speak
  As lover never spoke to one he loved.
How clear the west, unpinionable, and all gold,
As tho' to cleanse us for the coming of the stars!
    Now even we are worthy of the truth; —
    I, to lay bare, and thou, to hear.
But yet, the words may stab; nor am I brave —
    So, pr'ythee, turn from me thine eyes,
  Nor let me see thy perilous, curved mouth,
Crimson as flame, and cold as blooms at dawn.
    So. (My words seem shackled —
    Sluggish with frosty truth). . . .

    That moment long ago when thee I saw,
And straight the whole world 'came invisible,
    That time of passionate oblivion,
  Once seemed to me the incarnation time
Of love, the heaven-sent, the Paraclete!
    Thus have I told thee; thus believed.
      But, ignorant, I lied.
  No spirit of the Lord anointed paused
Within the portals of my heart on hallowed feet.
    Not that, but some young god,

With blown, bright hair and fillet golden, came,
And, stretching forth the blossoming rod of beauty,
    Upon me wrought a pagan spell.
  Not love, not love, — nor then, nor now!
If Christ should halt beside this spot to touch my hand,
  It would not be to claim my soul as friend;
But I should hear the sound of fearful things
    That rush into the sea.
  This fierce obsession of my waking hours,
  This visioning that makes night ecstasy,
  It is not love. And this the proof. —
Ah, heart's desire, should thy strong beauty fail
    As fails the beauty of the fields,
  Or foam blown where the seas are beachless,
  To me long, sweet forgetfulness would come,
And summer's ease, once known, now long ago.

  Thy words are music rich within mine ear,
But yet, I listen not if there be meaning in them.
    Thine eyes, like winter seas,
Dim grey, with thought of green and fear of blue,
  Thy listening eyes, immeasurably still —
  Oh, are they still with dreams, and sleep
  Deeper than waking? Or with the drowse
Of inner lassitude and sheer vacuity of soul?
    I dare not guess,
  But, careless, drink their cool, Circean sorcery.
  Hast thou a heart? I cannot say;
For, where it may not be I once did watch
A thought surge, flaming all thy wintry white
    To blossoming spring.

Mayhap, thy soul twines deep with God's.
Mayhap . . . I know
Thy body's whiteness and old Grecian grace . . .
As to one seeking glimpse of the huge sea,
Might come as hindrance on the slopes
An almond tree,
Leaning in ecstasy of petalled beauty, so
Betwixt thy soul and mine riseth alway
This barrier — thy loveliness!

A PAGE SINGS

    Where leads my way?
By trees that flutter in the wind,
      By fields half blind
With dew, by halls where I may find
      At afterday,
      Heathen or fay.

    I pass and sing.
With cool-eyed youth and all delight
      I am bedight —
From morning light to morning light
      Adventuring.
One song I sing.

    Beneath the blue,
The lithe trees lean my song to hear.
      It is so clear
Even their blytheness it can cheer —
      For fresh and true,
      'Tis all of you!

WINTER–FEAR

The rain has come.
Gone the empurpled air
Which hung upon the golden wreckage of the trees.
The rain has come,
And one no longer sees
The sun. The radiance that lay upon the vair
And crimson of the earth is vanishèd with these.

The wind is up.
It greits; nor dazzles now
The quiet lanes with ruined autumn's gorgeousness.
The wind is up,
But tho' the boughs confess
Its potency, of jeweled tribute they allow
No leaf. The earth, Danaë once, is treasureless.

Winter is come —
The night-cursed, fearful days,
Stainèd and blurred with tears and querulous with pain.
Winter is come,
And if my heart refrain
Most bitterly from backward looks when pitying stays
The sun, then, God! what agony these days of rain!

TO A MOCKING-BIRD: FROM TAORMINA

The nightingale has a golden heart,
    And a silver heart the wren;
But, oh, for me the bold, bright bird
    That sings with the heart of men!

His music is not of seas forlorn,
    His magic is not of tears;
From tilted throat his raptures float
    And tumble in laughter and jeers.

He does not cease when daylight dies,
    But he sings right on to the dark;
The stars or moon may die or swoon,
    In the drip of the rain — O hark!

He does not cease when spring is done,
    And his mate with love is fled;
A fairer thing than love or spring
    Is life. And the fall is red.

Sing, nightingales and silver wrens
    And fairy throats that can;
But the bird I love is the darling bird
    With the free, proud heart of a man.

AFTER READING THE RUBAIYAT

Still burning, let me cast the cup of youth aside,
    Or else, with one deep, purple draught,
Crush it and toss its unregretted pieces wide
To windwards, and the latter days abide.

What if the spicery of summer be forspent,
    And night's own argent madness gone?
The shining Bacchanal of youth was always rent
By cries the circling dark and stars had sent.

And tho' warm-lidded lechery was sweet, I knew
    The discontent of higher dreams,
And how the red-lipped sweetness changed and staled
    and grew
A thing the dewy dancers feared to view.

O loveliest of all the wreathèd revellers,
    Break, break the cup, the wine forswear.
Courageous, thee and me a lordlier vintage stirs —
The blood of life's unraptured warriors.

A WINTER'S NIGHT

The wind has reverenced the splendor of the night.
    Westward upon the green and saffron light
Of dusk it passed, with vasty wings and voice not low,
    Fleeing with awe the splendor of the night.

Were I the wind to-night, the tangled stars and snow
    My aweless wings' unfettered might would know.
O joy, the trancèd splendor of the air to shake
    And starward hurl like spray the errant snow!

Ah, for the tyranny of furious wings, to wake
    Superb, this ecstasy of calm; to slake
My passion-winnowed heart with tempests' windy woe!
    I would to-night the storms were all awake!

AT PARTING

And so we part!
You with your vague, sweet smile,
I with a breaking heart;
You to your vague, sweet ways,
I where the failures start.

We lingered long!
You for mere idleness,
I for your mouth like song;
You for the flattery,
I for your beauty strong.

Our lips' last touch!
Yours cold as mere consent,
Mine colder were there such.
And you will never know,
And I have known too much.

. . .

Parting sublime!
Already you've forgot,
I will forget in time.
You sigh without regret,
And I have heart to rhyme.

BEFORE DAWN

Breath of the dawn, breath of the dawn,
Breathe on my heart of thine eagerness.
Up from the sea, youthful with thee,
        Be drawn
For a spell and a healing to me
        In my stress.

With the shining of silver yet on thy feet,
With the fleeing of stars that are flameless fleet,
With the cool of the sea for the cool of thine eyes,
        Arise
        And come to my need!
From the grey of the unstarred eastern skies
        Oh, speed!

Up from the sea, up from the sea,
Come with thine eagerness, girlishly;
Sweep with the quiver and gleaming of thee
Dark from my heart like dew from the lawn;
With the cool of thy coming, half stars and half sun,
Deliver my soul from the deeds that are done —
Breath of the dawn, breath of the dawn,
        Purify me.

LONGING

At last the sunset and the quietness;
   The iron clutch of day loosened at last.
  Here where the sky is limpid loveliness
     And depth on depth of peace, I may forget
The fretful work-a-day and midgy round of things . . .
    A smothered pain the long, long day.
Nor does forgetting come with dark and nights of dream;
   But sweet with pain and filmèd tenderness
    This hour of the pity of all things. . . .
Grey as slow tears, the dusk blurs out the trees;
   The colors ebb beneath the western marge;
     And homing come the birds —
      Not singly come they, but,
    With throated happiness, together.
But we no more shall come together home,
   Nor hear their twittering gusts,
Nor watch the deep west come more deep
    Till we behold the stars,
So bright they must but now have wept.
    Oh, for one hour to-night,
   One little hour with you —
    To touch your hand —
To lean within the halo of your perfume —
   To watch, as those sweet many times,
    Together, love, the young, white moon,
Like some strange petal blown into our round of space
   From out the cool abysms of the night,

Where unknown blossoms bloom for unknown eyes
    To gaze upon in wistfulness. . . .
    A little while to watch,
    And then, together, home.

PHAON IN HADES

To-day the very dead would love his face;
And, loving them, I wish that to their place
Of woe his feet might find awhile the way,
And ease them with perfection for a space.
His beauty is so beautiful to-day.

As, when its freight of dew is blown away,
The grass uprises, so would they uprise,
Those ancient dead, and shake their anguish grey,
Breathing his coolness and his glad surprise
As 'twere the blow and glittering of day.

Ashine with clinging petals and late tears,
Sweet with aroma of Sicilian green,
I see the dear, dear dead make way and lean
To catch the summer of his mouth, the sheen
Of laughter in those eyes that wisdom fears.

And, ah! Persephone! She hath forgot
The pallor and the poppied heaviness —
Upon her wine-red heart her hand is hot.
If thus the very dead, 'twere sure excess
Of blame, were I to love his beauty less!

GIRGENTI

So many here have struggled, fought the fight!
   Life after life so many here have flung
As incense to the gods, that served — for what
   Save Cerberus' toll to nothingness?
   Of what avail to them, to us,
   Their gaunt resistance and their trust?
Across the clear, sad light of centuries,
Their epitaph reveals what line of comfort?
Those that with lit, courageous eyes opposed
The mean, the merely earth, the less than highest,
Was recompense or special profit theirs?
   Did their names less profoundly plumb
       The chasms of oblivion
         Than theirs that never fought,
         But, lightly submissive, spread
        The purple for their summer hearts
        Within the garden's cool,
Called for the golden cups, the snowy wine,
   The honey-comb, and Aphrodite's flutes?
To which was happiness the booner comrade?
Sweeter than chaplets hold you sweat and blood!
   Than easy pomp, strife and hot tears!
     Which likelier served the gods?
   Behold the gods of both in ambered death
     Of fairy tales and poets' guile!
      Which hold in heritage
Elysian meadows and eternal May?

Poor trade, indeed, hoped immortality
For hot lips and the certain spring!
Ah! but the nobler struggle did bequeath
   Impetus, blossom-bearing warmth unto
That blind and mighty impulse to perfection —
   The race's slow, incessant upward surge!
      Dreams! dreams! About, about, behold
      Their bastard-souled successors,
      Legitimate in blood alone!
Here once were millions; gazing hence, one saw
The high-hung walls, the teeming market place,
   The colors and the colonnades,
The curving city's brilliant amplitude. . . .
   There hangs upon that northern crag,
   As some dirt-wasp had hovelled there,
   The drab inheritor of all that purpose;
Slattern of villages, where sat the lily-crowned!
     Golden Girgenti!
   Of soft Sicilian cities goldenest!
    Gone, all gone thy gold,
Save where the rhythm of the ripened fields
   Sweeps mellowing to the sea;
Save where the lonely temples lift their pride,
   And on their maimed and desecrated fronts
   The evening light lays heavenly pure hands.
Gone thy gold; thy beauty, childless, gone;
Gone alike the strugglers and the strife.
Only the bland, unflashing blue, the Libyan,
   Holds yet its immemorial loveliness.
   Thus from the lofty temple steps at gaze,
   My thoughts came faltering.

But my proud heart leaped up in glittering mail
And called:
>Tho' the gods be dead or never were;
Tho' death blow out the flame and soul be dust;
>Tho' generation follow generation
>Level, no higher footing gained, no hope
>Broad day will sometime flood the race
>Upon some mountain won with agony;
Tho' all dissolve and leave no mist of gold —
>Yet vision only and the strife therefor
>>Shall I accept as life!
If here, across this present's windy peak, I gaze
>Back, back across the infinite years,
>And forward thro' the infinite to be —
>Above the human rabble, past the soft
Guzzlers against the fertile breasts of life,
>I see, I do behold, how proudly, them
Whom blind nobility, heroic uselessness,
Impelled to scorn all acquiescence, brute
And easy; to strike to the blood's last crimson for
>The dream of their own making;
>Defenders, tho' creators, of their own
>Divinity; soldiers in sweat, in blood,
>>Before the mouth of death.
>So long as one remain, but one,
To shout the battle cry and take no quarter,
So long the velvet ease of life is infamous,
So long I stand with him and beard the world!
Girgenti, O Girgenti, vanished all thy sons!
>And only spring with equal glory spreads
Across thy hills its billows of deep bloom.

Empedocles, thy loveliest, is gone;
And Dædalus is dead; his wings no more
Shall darken up the east or shake the sea;
Nor any make return whose name thy mouth
  Smiled to repeat. Yet not to them
  My heart gives hail across the grave.
    Oh, not to them whose heralding
  Sufficient heaven gave to their attempt.
  But to thy sons, that, silently,
    Oblivion-crowned,
  Battled as tho' the very gods made part,
And from their golden ramparts called applause.
  Them do I hail across the heavy mold;
And them unborn, foredoomed to like red death,
Whose swords submit not chance, nor fate, nor flesh. . . .
  My brothers, proud, tho' unworthy, let me stand with you
    In stubborn rank against the wall of doom,
    Opposing meek acceptance of the world;
  Scornful of scorn and vileness and black sloth;
  Battling, we know not why; dying, we care not how;
  Glimpsing our kinship with the farther stars;
    Defeated always — but how splendidly!

THE HAPPY ISLES

How comes the spring in those far lands of yours?
    Tremulous as here — and full of wings?
    Full, too, of secrets and the hint
        Of half divine events?
    Do twilights there unfold
Blue shadow petals to the swarm of stars?
And does the hem of rapture darkness wears
    Glisten, as here, with tears?

    This hour that we loved most,
My long forgetting like a garment falls.
    How long away! From you how long!
        Failure and tears and strife,
    The intermittent bubbling up
        Of that deep loneliness
    All know, yet know not to resist —
These come, but coming, wake not surely in my heart
        Its lack of you.

But yours, yours always, are the Happy Isles!
    Their transient, fortuitous discovery —
    Rarer each year that sears and falls —
        Brings back the need of you.
And every failing breath sent from their shores
        Seems meant for two.
    Let but the darkling hour as now
Move mystical upon the tides of spring,

And from the vague horizon's verge they rise.
    The air is unheard music that we knew;
Ahead, familiarly, the purple shallows shine;
       I turn, I turn
    To whom alone with me is sovereign there,
        And, missing you,
    Miss, too, the opal of their magic coves,
    And scant the fugitive, bland hour.

But no! that thought would shade your eyes,
    Tho' fresh with immortality.
Oh, think not you can ever bring me pain —
Or pain such only as clear sunsets cast;
Their shining wings uplift us and their peace seems home,
    But sadness is their soul,
And all their lustral loveliness wells up from tears.

Perhaps, there, too, in those far lands of yours,
Springtime comes flowing like a tide of dreams,
      Mysterious, on bluer wings,
Laving in magic more profound the curve of lovelier
      shores.
      Yet, even there, perhaps,
    Your unaccustomed eyes yearn back
    Across the spirit-footed ocean of the air,
    And you are homesick for the earth,
Twilight, and stars that are not worlds but flowers —
    Homesick, perhaps, tho' Paradise be yours,
      For me and for those isles. . . .
    They fade; the world returns,
    And with them fades

The conjured vision of your biding place.
    Soon may they come again;
Soon; on the waters blue of twilight,
    Tremulous, full of wings,
The purple of unrisen stars about their base,
And on their crest the calm of sunset.

EPILOGUE

O God, author of song
  And of the will to righteousness,
Thee have I loved in guise of him,
  The golden-haired, the beautiful,
  The incense-tainted leader of the Nine,
With dim, averted eyes and prescience of pain —
Knowing Thee frail and perishable, fit for youth.

The gardens of the air were mine to walk with Thee,
    Dewed with the stars,
  Swept with the tinted splendors of the suns.
  Yet was the bliss too blissful to commend,
  And Thou, I knew, wert half divine, no more.
    Thro' the live luxury
    Of that aerial rapture always
  Crashed the vast battle sounds of earth,
  Where, tho' the many died, myself died not,
  Where, tho' the many bled, myself unwounded went.
    The pagan god, Thyself half-seen,
      Is not enough, O God!
  Here, on the breaking verge of youth,
Secureless from the fringes of the forward storm,
  I face the riven grey and call to Thee,
    O God of righteousness, to Thee!
Must I forswear song and the darling rapture,
Thy gifts, tho' taintless of the earth, yet beautiful?
And bend me to the living of the life, half-armed,

Lacking not valiance, but the accoutrements wherewith
    Valiance may save itself from scorn?

O God, hear Thou my faith which is as rock:
    Thou art! All else is circumstance,
        Random and unessential incident —
      Save this: in me Thou art.
And so my moment wheels to its sure end
Huge with divinity, its orbit as the sun's,
    Accounted and accountable as all
The chaos-floating, golden universe.
        But mine to mar;
    Mine to deliver unto death
True to the disposition of its essence,
Or in fulfillment bastard utterly.
      Eternal Thou; but I
Swift-passing, in the passing powerful
    Myself to darken with deliberate choice.
      One life, but one, is mine.
      I would not have it pass
    Failing its high, potential utmost,
A quivering of music-shaken strings — no more.

Giver of bliss and pain, of song and prayer,
    Thou God that dost demand
Single allegiance of the soul that sees
    Thee dual only and at enmity —
  Hearken my choice, my supplication hark.
    Tear out the rapture and the wings —
      Take back thy gift of song —
Take, take the madness of the olive and the vine

With all their ecstasies, unless they be
Not oil for gleaming of the games and clustered gold,
   Not wine for leafy laughter of the feast,
But aid and chrismed healing for the wounds
   Of them that smitten lie on that broad way
   Known to the dusty sandals from Samaria.
Crush Thou, O God, the petalled crimson of my life,
   So Thou but mold the remnant clay
      To shape not all unworthy of the Thee in me.

PART II

IN APRIL ONCE, AND OTHER POEMS

I
SICILIANA

PART II

GURBILGEN, AND OTHER POEMS

I
SICHNAY

Regretting that anything which bears his name should not be lovelier, but knowing that with him there would be no regret to find it here inscribed, I dedicate this poem of which we spoke so often to Major WILLIAM SINKLER MANNING. *It was given him to die as only the best deserve, gloriously, in battle, leading his troops in the attack on Hill 378, November the sixth, 1918. Life, as we know it, lost a lover of all that was beautiful and right, and I, my dear friend.*

IN APRIL ONCE

Characters { DAVID   SERLE DE LANLARAZON
GUIDO   FELICE
HUGO   GUARDS }

THE YEAR A.D. 1220; *a castle near Florence. A court on top of one of the bastions. To the right, a crenelated parapet over which a glimpse is had of an April landscape — hills, poplars, deep yellow sunlight. Fifty feet below, unseen, runs the road between Florence and the north. At the back, the walls of the castle and a wide doorway leading into the interior.*

During the action, late afternoon changes to sunset, sunset to twilight, and at the end it is almost dark.

As the scene opens, the sound of retreating horses' hoofs is heard. DAVID *is standing on the parapet watching. He is twenty-two, strongly built, blond, with blue, wide-set eyes and sullen, brooding expression, simply dressed, with coat of mail and sword. He whistles and* GUIDO'S *head appears at a window.*

GUIDO *is of the same age, a trifle taller and more slender, very dark, beautiful, full of high spirits and humorous gusto. His dark eyes are vivid and changing. He is elegantly dressed as a courtier.*

DAVID *throws him a rope with a rope ladder attached.* GUIDO *fastens it and descends to the court.*

GUIDO (*as he descends*). Thou are the knightliest jailer that ever
      stood
    Betwixt light heart and the free world. Were I
    The Emperor, thou shouldst be seneschal
    Of my Sicilian Joyous Guard, instead
    Of jailer and henchman to the Florentines.
    There lie the fragrant spaces, the glistening air,
    The very troubadour and gypsy time o' year;
    And here am I, hindered and snared, mewed up,
    Because, forsooth, I sing the Emperor's songs,
    Set off his colors, bear his pleasantries
    To some adorèd lady of Provence,
    To which your gross and choleric Florentines
    Attach significance and secret import.
    Jailer, the very spring hath need of me,
    And that sweèt southward-wending road
    Would fringe itself, I swear, with gayer tulips
    Were I but lilting to its guidance south.
    Couldn't you let me out, David?
DAVID. No, I could not.
GUIDO. If I should wheedle you; if I should be
    The very most delightfulest young squire
    And love you as my heart's most boon companion?
    Say, you slept and dreamed of good Saint Peter,
    What harm, if, when you woke, your keys were gone,
    By chance or miracle — or merely me?
DAVID. Were you Lord Jesus I'd not let you out.

GUIDO.   I do almost surmise, somehow, I'm still
       This prison's darling guest, and like to be
       A many a month. Jesu, what waste, what waste!
DAVID.   O can't you see? I must not let you go!
       The Florentines to me are nothing,
       But I made oath to serve them faithfully
       And they believed me.
GUIDO.   Indeed, I do see, David.
       Why, if you should accede to my keen urgence,
       I would not go . . .
       At least, I think I would not go, perhaps.
DAVID.   But, truly, are you so unhappy here?
GUIDO.   In prison! and not most wretched! . . . How can you ask?
       Yet now I come to think of it . . . David,
       That is the loveliest window in my cell!
       Sometimes, when the sky is blurry yellow,
       Just before dawn, you know,
       You'd think there were a thousand birds outside;
       And in my bed I lie, all shimmery,
       Thinking delicious things
       I never can remember afterwards.
       And when, at last, I'm up and washed and wake,
       There is the tender sunlight in long sweeps,
       And the rose-colored hills, and the youthful poplars,
       And the first green, so faint
       You fear to look at it right steadily
       Lest it should mist and melt away.
       It's splendid, David.
       But — now I know why I am miserable!
       Think of the things I miss cooped up in here.
       Adventures by the thousand wait out there!

When we rode up from Sicily, the page and I,
We killed a robber, saw the Pope,
Danced in a masquerade, fasted two days,
Composed ten roundelays (in the vernacular),
And kissed a princess on the cheek.

DAVID (*impressed*). A brave existence! But I am free
To take my share of it and never do.

GUIDO. That's strange — you stay here willingly! But why?

DAVID. Adventures do not wait out there — for me.

GUIDO. Absurd! If we could only go right now —
Think, lad, of the seas unsailed, the tourneys missed,
The battles others fight, the roads not cantered on;
That very road, so plain and real and white,
Leads out to courts and castles of romance.
A road like that led to Emmaus once.
Why, now I think it would not be so hard
To meet Lord Jesus walking there alone,
Watching His springtime glisten up,
And humming to Himself! Yonder He comes!

DAVID. Hush, Guido! Hush, you fool!

GUIDO. But look! The sun is on his hair! He's very young.

(DAVID *goes to the edge, looks down, and turns back.*)

(A *voice singing on the road.*)

God's lark at morning I would be,
I'd set my heart within a tree
Close to His bed and sing to Him
   Right merrily
   A sunrise hymn.

DAVID. A monk.

GUIDO. He's stopped by Tonio's donkey.

DAVID. Means to steal him, likely.

VOICE. Brother Ass, I give you good den. As I came down the road desiring greatly of your company, I did bethink me of the noble part you played, times past, in Holy Writ. Whereon said I, to the next ass I meet I will impart the goodly thoughts vouchsafèd me. But, prithee, Brother Ass, let not thine ears recede upon thy nape, nor thy long face betoken grief of soul! These are *good* tidings that I bear. (*Laughs.*) Harken! Christ's Father, which is God, once spoke from out the belly of an ass, astounding much the prophet that bestrode him, and honoring your kinsman and his children's children, even to you. And later, another of your ancestors bore Christ Himself into Jerusalem. Wherefore, say I, you should be prouder than the horse, more praiseful than the bird, more — but that's enough!

GUIDO. Bravo, Sir Orator!

VOICE. I would have sermoned twice as long had I but known two asses heard.

GUIDO (*laughing*). Your hermit's frock mates not with your light page's tongue.

VOICE. Nay, Francis says the Lord loves best the happy heart.

GUIDO. And who is Francis?

VOICE. God-a-lack!
Not know the little poor man of Assisi?
He says he is mere man like us. Perhaps —
But one in whom the breath of God has not yet cooled.

GUIDO. And you?

VOICE. I am but one of many brethren!
We teach God's love and holy poverty,
But first we love and are ourselves most poor.
Come with us!

GUIDO. Are all as happy as you look?

Voice.   You should hear Brother Francis sing!
         Bethink you, friend, if this is God's dear world,
         And we His children, if the years we have
         To do His will are few, so few, O think
         How wasted is all work not done for Him.
         Ponder these things, young heart, and come with us . . .
         And Jesus keep you — and the woeful ass!

             (*Sings as he goes down the road.*)

             At night I'd be God's troubadour.
             Beneath His starry walls I'd pour
             Across the moat such roundelays
                 He'd love me sure,
                 And maybe, praise.

Guido (*watching him disappear*).   I think I'd almost like to go with
         him.
David.   That's not Emmaus road. He'll not meet God.
Guido.   Isn't it strange how God is easy to
         Forget? And to remember too! Whole days
         I go so brimful of the bliss of things
         I never think of Him. And then He comes,
         Quite naturally, and not at all displeased —
         Perhaps a summer night scattered with stars,
         Or far off in the dusk a sweet song heard,
         Or when you're lonely and you want someone
         To kiss you, to hold you close, and let you cry;
         Or sometimes when the splendors seem to rain
         And sunset skies quiver and rock with gold,
         And voices call you and you hear your own
         Answering back, swearing to go crusading,
         Or to a hermit's cell, or on some quest.

It's strange . . . But He doesn't worry me a bit!
DAVID. I hope you always find Him so, Guido.
But you've not sworn to go on the crusades?
GUIDO. Not truly sworn, just to myself.
Zounds! what a knightly quest! Worth all the blood
Spilled, and the failures! Let's go together, David.
DAVID. Not worth, I swear, the life of one good man,
Although it won the Sepulchre.
GUIDO. By all the saints! I don't believe you think that!

(DAVID *is silent.*)

'Tis natural we should revere His tomb —
Unless you have no faith that He is God?
David, do you, perchance, know other gods
Besides the old ones of the Trinity?
DAVID. No. Do you?
GUIDO. Lots of 'em! Only listen!
Pallas, Persephone, Olympian Zeus,
Hermes, Artemis, Ganymede, —
DAVID. And what became of them? Crucified too?
GUIDO. Oh, no; somehow they were forgotten.
DAVID. You jest.
I thought you'd found, perhaps, another hope.
GUIDO. I'll tell you just the way I learned of them.
You see, the Emperor wished his pages taught
All wisdom of all countries and all times
So they might adepts in delightfulness
Become, to grace the earthly paradise
He'd made his court. I was his favorite page.
Oh, it was fairy stuff, that life of ours!
We'd sit or lie or sprawl about the fountain
In Monreale's high-built orange-court,

A score of laughing pages, olive-hued,
And gold-haired Enzio, the Emperor's son.
'Twould be sun-splashed up there, not hot nor cool,
But always thick with perfume from the trees,
And dim with water sounds and litanies
That friars pacing in the cloisters told.
And, morning long, an Arab sage would read
The precious parchments from Byzantium.
You've seen, David, some arch half hid in flowers
That winds and butterflies and birds blow through —
Well, such an arch I've always been till now,
With all the fragrance, rapture, melody
Of all the world just blowing through, lightly.
From those old parchments we young pages learned
Of men long dead who seemed to us ourselves,
Only more wise and radiant and fair,
Who lived in Greece once, loved with their whole strength
The earth and sun, and offered up their prayers
To many cool-eyed gods with rippling names.
But placid gods they were that never worked!

DAVID. Forgotten gods in books to me are nothing.
GUIDO. For everyday they're not as good as Christ.
They are just beautiful; you pray to them,
They hardly hear; you'd never make them weep.
Of course you go to Christ when you are hurt,
Or when you feel — like a young tree in bloom!
DAVID. Do you feel that way all the time?
GUIDO (*laughing*). Mostly!

(*Goes up on a parapet. The sunset is cloudless — transparencies of
intense color.*)

God, God, how beautiful Your world is! Sometimes
It seems to me I should do something noble,
Some deed You'd love, to truly show my thanks . . .
David, this riding up and down the world
In scarlet hose is not enough, think you?
Others leave all they love to fight for Christ,
Or take the sea to find new lands for Him,
Or quit the dear society of men
To seek for angels in the wilderness.
They say that in the north, whole villages
Are sometimes struck with the wild thought of God,
And careless of their personal, sharp needs,
Give up their all to build Him palaces
Of blue and emerald glass and marble lace.
I'd hate another man to have
A goodlier soul than I! . . .
But how diversely we are lovable!
We must be quite a pleasure to our Lord.

A *voice screaming.*   Son of David, have mercy on me!

GUIDO (*terribly startled*).   What was that cry!

DAVID.   The madman's scream.
    They burned out both his eyes for some old crime
    And he went mad. His cell is under us.
    Sometimes he screams like that.

GUIDO (*horrified*).   Then there are other prisoners in this place?

DAVID.   From that bright room of yours you never see
    The ghastly crew that I am captain of.
    But there are those beneath your very feet
    In dungeon after dungeon, who will die
    And never see the sun. This is a hive
    Of misery. You only heard one buzz.

GUIDO.   They never come up here?

DAVID.   Only for you I break the prison's rules.

GUIDO.   Who are they, down — down there?

DAVID.   Thieves, politicians, murderers, and such.
Mostly they die. Two only have been here
For many years.

GUIDO.   What crimes did they commit?

DAVID.   One's a pirate, that roars and sings and curses;
Hugo by name. He begs to tell me his adventures.

GUIDO.   I'd listen till he'd told me the last one!
I'd like to see that pirate . . . and the other?

DAVID.   A heretic.

GUIDO (*laughing*).   So's the Emperor!

DAVID.   His is the deepest dungeon of them all,
No sun, no breath of air, just slime and stench.
Ten years ago when first they flung him there
His tongue was brash and peppery, they say,
His body broad and big, a fighting man's.
But he has rotted in that stinking hole.
I shade my lantern when I bring his food.

GUIDO.   Horrible! Horrible! Does he cry out?

DAVID.   No. . . . Though he is heretic, he has
A God whose name he praises and whose strength
Implores. To me he never makes complaint;
But once he asked,
"Has Albi's faith yet spread to Italy?"

GUIDO.   Albi! The home of heretics!

DAVID.   And once, "Is Simon dead?"

GUIDO.   David, let's give a holiday to him
And to my pirate,
And bring them here to talk to us.

DAVID. You could not stand the sight of him; his flesh
    Is crumbled off, or fetid, white and stale.
    They gave him for his faith the lepers' cell.
GUIDO. God! God! Leave him down there!
DAVID. Yet I could hide him in a dead monk's cowl,
    And, while the guards are absent, let them both
    Come here to breathe the light and air once more.
    You could guard one while I'd go fetch the other.
GUIDO. If both must come, bring up the pirate first,
    So I may be alone with him — not with that other!
DAVID. But *could* you guard the pirate? He's strong and —
GUIDO (*indignant*). By God! Could I? Because I dress in silk,
    And sing a snatch, mayhap, and speak of birds
    And blossoms and such amorous, frail things,
    Thou thinkest me weakling!
    With one good broadsword and a mind to it,
    I'd guard secure a host of pirates! . . . 'Swounds!
              (*Sees a sword lying on the bench.*)
    Lend me that sword! . . . On guard! . . . Now, all your skill!

(*They fence. A sudden twist, and* GUIDO *catches* DAVID'*s sword with his, whirling it into the air.* GUIDO *in high spirits runs up to the battlement.*)

GUIDO. That old Sicilian trick!
    Now who is master here? Free, free, O world!
    Now could I cut the gold-haired jailer's head off
    And steal his keys and rush out to the road,
    And lark it down to Sicily again.
DAVID (*repressing his admiration*). I'd love to be your battle brother once,
    And, standing by your side, strike down a hundred!

Guido. David, you almost angered me. Bring up the prisoners!

(*Exit* David. Guido *sits with his feet hanging over the parapet and sings.*)

    O, shall I sail the rough, bright sea,
        And on some glittering morn
    Blow with the wind that blows so free,
    Up to a strange and a fair countree,
        And wind on my silver horn?

    Or shall I loosen my long, grey lance,
        Leap my stallion astride,
    And down the mottled wood-paths prance
    To capture the city of romance
        That the golden cloud-banks hide?

    Sing heigh, sing ho! The bliss of being,
        The glory of days that rush,
    So much to be doing, hearing, seeing,
    With spring foaming up, and winter a-fleeing,
        And the rose of youth in blush!

(*Enter* David *with* Hugo, *enormous, red-bearded, this side of middle age.* David *goes out.*)

Guido. Men say you have been in your day
    The fearfulest rover of the seas.
Hugo. They said not half. My soul can count
    More dreadful deeds than the Old Man of the Mountain,
    And more are yet to do.
Guido. You've sailed, perhaps, the western sea?
Hugo. Western and eastern, Pontic and Caspian!
Guido. And seen the marvels of the world's grey edge?

Hugo. All of them. Once for twenty days I sailed
   Beyond the gateways of the world into the west.
   The winds had voices like the damned,
   There was no sun; the sea was like —
Guido. The flameless, grey, upheaving boundaries of hell
   Where drift those truckling spirits who in life
   Shunned the affray.
Hugo. A-hem! Have you been there?
Guido. Well, as it were . . . Go on. As you roved up
   The heliotrope, soft sea of Greece
   Did you, perchance, catch glimpses of
   The women of the sea?
Hugo. A many a one.
Guido. How looked they?
Hugo. Sleek and bosomed high.
Guido. What color were their eyes?
Hugo. I noted not their eyes.
Guido. Blind fool! But never mind, I know.

(DAVID *enters with the heretic, who wears the white habit of a monk,
   the cowl over his head hiding his face. He can hardly walk;* DAVID
   *supports him. He pauses, dazed by the late sunlight, then sits on
   the bench at back center, silently.*)

Guido (*nervously covering the embarrassment of their entrance*).
   David, this man hath seen the women of the sea,
   And found them fair.
Hugo.   But not as fair by half
   As those of earth. Jesu, no sight of one
   For these damned years I've rotted here;
   And there's a many a town on many a shore
   Where lasses weep and beat their breasts for me.

GUIDO. Hast thou adventured in the further south
   Where spicier seas
   Break on the carven shores of lovelier lands,
   Where women, sultry-hued as summer's myrtle,
   With half-closed, tawny eyes that never close,
   Await far sails of vaster glittering
   That bear superbly to their attared arms
   More bright-haired, iron-chested lovers
   Out of the north?
HUGO.   To the neighboring isles,
   And there I'll harbor on my next adventure.
GUIDO. I love thee, Hugo.
   Thou art the most heroicalest liar
   Leewards of greedy hell.
HUGO. A man must be to keep apace with you.
   But you, I swear, are not a common jailer.
   What is your land and lineage?
GUIDO. My home, Palermo; my estate, the Emperor's love.
HUGO. A courtly knight! A silken squire of dames!
   I wager you are served with jades a-plenty.
DAVID. Do you know love, real love, Guido?
GUIDO. The gods have not vouchsafed me that transmuting test,
   But I have longed for Circe and,
   Remembering her sties, still longed.
HUGO. Who may that lady be?
GUIDO. A witch of qualities.
HUGO. As?
GUIDO. Shadow robes that cling, and shadow eyes,
   Warm, tulip-tinted mouth, all else Carrara whiteness.
   The prodigal son was hireling to her, and forgot
   Even his father, eating of her husks.

DAVID.   Is she the lady, Guido, has a house
    In Florence, where the other jailers now
    Drink of her wine and — eat her husks?
GUIDO.   The same, the same! I'm glad you're here, David.
    It's easy to forget they're husks in April;
    Then lechery is iridescent-winged,
    Mere throbbing up of leafy sun-drawn sap;
    Mere clinging of frail lips; mere mockery
    Of light-intoxicated eyes,
    That thrill together under lowered lids —
    Half irresistible and wholly sweet.
    And yet — I'm glad we're here, David.
HUGO.   If I were free this afternoon,
    I know a harlot's house in Florence —
GUIDO.   Ah, there it is! Always the same!
    There's nothing this side love but vileness;
    And without either there's such rapture i' the world.
    Let's keep it so, O jailer of my heart.
    Forget the sirens for a while, thou bearded beast,
    And tell us brackish tales of the wild sea.
HUGO.   I have no notion who the sirens be,
    Nor Circe, nor what means
    That womanish, springtime talk of yours.
    I doubt me if ye know a broadsword from a dirk.
    You could not understand a lively man's adventures.
GUIDO.   David, I think we hold in vile captivity
    The fieriest brigand that ever slew — with words,
    The doughtiest sailor that ever sailed — by breath.
    Of course, he may have pulled a harbor yawl,
    Or held for ransom valiantly a capture of sardines.
    Nay, more, I grant, with faithful henchmen by,

   He may have subjugated, cheese and all,
   An irate granny-dame, sail set for market.
Hugo. Body of Christ!
   Shall flesh and blood endure this popinjay,
   This thing of silk, this — Before you came,
   A red worm thing into the bellowing world,
   I'd waded knee-deep in fresh human blood,
   Slain Greeks a hundred, sacked the vizier's harem,
   Gathered a hamper full of sacred bones,
   And, drunk on sacramental wine, sailed back
   To Venice with two span of iron horses.
Guido (*delighted*). You on the gorgeous Byzantine crusade?
   Did you not catch the tale from other lips
   When you were linkboy on the Grand Canal?
Hugo. These very hands, thou saucy innocent,
   Have purpled with imperial bastards' blood;
   These eyes saw Dandolo's fleet assault the walls,
   The Greeks' vermilion tent and molten oil,
   The mangonels and catapult and bridge.
   When André of Urboise dashed through the breach
   I followed, and 'twas I first lit the torch
   That fired a thousand houses, where old men
   And slattern women howled and cursed and burned!
   That was a real crusade! Gold, wine
   And women whose consent the sword could always win.
   These are dull times! Hey, silent monk!
   Preach Christ and war against the infidel!
   That's the brave life! With heathen gold
   And heathen concubines, who would not fight
   For Christ?
David. Now would you be crusader, Guido?

GUIDO. The beast!

HUGO (*in high fettle*).   Then I've another crusade tale for you.
    Sweet Christ! 'Twas a divine burlesque!
    Of all that crossed the sea not one returned
    Save me, their leader.

GUIDO.   Your lies grow wearisome.

DAVID (*with premonition and repression*). Say on, say on!

HUGO.   It was in France, near such a day as this;
    We idled in the southern harbor there,
    Our seven empty hulls against the quays.
    I do remember well, 'twas afternoon.
    On deck we slept beneath the sails or diced
    And wished the night would come. Then suddenly,
    From the hill crest where the wide street came down,
    We heard a shout, and, looking up, beheld —
    You'll know I'm lying now — it looked a dream —
    A thousand children

              (DAVID *leaps up and stands white and taut.*)
              with flowers on their heads
    And crosses in their hands and wreaths and banners;
    And when they saw us or the sea or something,
    They fell upon their knees with prayers and cries,
    Kissed one another, wept, went mad with joy.
    While we, chap-fallen, watched their antics, up
    They sprang, broke into hymns to Jesus and
    Came down the sloping street right to the sea.

GUIDO.   But why?

HUGO.   Baccho! It was the Crusade of the Children,
    And they were marching with their songs and flowers
    To take Christ's Sepulchre!

GUIDO.   What's in Jerusalem?

Hugo. Yea, verily.

Guido. But that was France!

Hugo. They came to us and said, "We're almost there;
Dear friends, we know, for we have marched so long;
And Christ has sent you here with seven ships
To ferry us across the sea." Whereon,
They knelt to us and called us, "Brothers in Christ,"
"Seamen of God," "Our Lady's mariners."
It had astounded you.

Guido. But so you were!
You took them to the Holy Tomb of Christ?

Hugo. Thou fool! That night we spent apart in council.
Next day, our scheme complete, we went to them
And swore to bear them to the Sepulchre.

Guido. I knew you would, our Lady's mariner!

Hugo. We herded them aboard our seven ships
And sailed for Alexandria — a golden freight!

Guido. Why there, and not unto Jerusalem?

Hugo. Children are precious to the infidel!
We sold the last one to the Turk; not one returned!
And there they do remain to this good hour,
Their slaves and concubines!

(David, *with a terrible cry, flings himself on* Hugo, *hurls him to the floor, strangles him.* Guido *with difficulty pulls him off.*)

Guido. Which is his cell?

David. To the right, the last.

(David *lies sobbing on the floor, while* Guido *takes* Hugo *out and returns.*)

Guido. There is some wickedness I had not guessed.

DAVID (*beside himself*).   I was one! I was one!
GUIDO.   What do you mean?
DAVID.   I was a child-crusader! The dog! The dog!
　　Then they, too, failed. No man had heard their fate.
　　I thought they sailed and reached the Sepulchre!
　　There is no justice and no right,
　　No pity and no kindness in the world!
　　Only the vile things prosper and live on.
　　Where is your God?
GUIDO.   I know not. I know nothing . . . But you —
　　Were you a child-crusader there in France?
DAVID.   Oh, no. Listen, Guido! Here's my life!

(DAVID *pauses to control himself, then proceeds with suppressed passion.*)

　　I was a shepherd boy beyond the Rhine.
　　A hilltop was my home. All summer there
　　I'd watch my flocks about me pasturing.
　　I could throw a stone and hit the road below me;
　　It was the road that led out to the world.
　　All day I'd lie and watch from the deep grass
　　The marvelous people passing — troubadours
　　With viol da gambas on their backs and singing;
　　Fat priests and friars, sometimes a cardinal,
　　And green and scarlet pages, little like me, —
　　I'd halloa down to them — and then the knights,
　　Always the noble knights with flashing mail
　　And retinues of stalwart men-at-arms.
　　The proudest-seeming always journeyed south,
　　Seeking Christ's Sepulchre, they said. They said
　　The infidels had made it theirs somehow,

Ruined and fouled and desecrated it;
And if God's knights could capture it again,
The sins o' the world would pass, and every sorrow,
And likely Christ would come again unto His own,
And somehow there were wings through all the air
In those first days. In the deep silence when
The sun stood still at noon and the flocks slept,
I'd hear, I thought, the angels all about me;
They walked among my sheep upon my hill.
And something always was about to break
Between another world and me.
I waited and was sure, some day, quite soon,
A glory would come true and I would kneel
I' the grass and see the Lord before me, close,
Yes, close enough to touch and talk to. Then one day
I found what I'd been wishing for so long.
Down on the road, far off, behind the hill,
I heard a hundred voices singing, not
Gleemen or pages, but like seraphim.
I knelt and waited, and the sheep were still.
Louder the singing grew and louder, then
Around the hillside into the sun they burst,
A host of children, a heavenly host,
With crosses in their hands and on their breasts.
They called to me and I came down and left my flock
And went with them, a soldier of the Christ. . . .
Guido, Guido, Guido, it was not fair!
We were so sure of God, we meant so well!
He let us starve and rot among the fields,
He lost us in the snow and ice of mountains,
We died, and died, and died, but still pushed on,

For we were only children and believed.
GUIDO. And those that did not die?
DAVID.   Half-frozen, starved,
   We staggered from the dreadful mountain pass
   And saw beneath us in the sunlight Italy.
   We thought it was the Promised Land. In tears,
   With arms around the weaker ones, we hurried
   Down the great mountain side to meet the Christ.
GUIDO. If only this could be a lie or dream!
DAVID. We knew the end was surely near. We wove
   Garlands and wreaths to lay upon His Tomb.
   Our leader was a lad named Nicholas —
   When souls are sacreder than his they will
   Not take the flesh! . . . One night he called us round
   And climbed upon a gateway in our midst
   And spoke to us.
   His face shone in the dark.
   He said, a final test the Lord had laid —
   Across our path He'd stretched the mighty sea.
   The children, terrified, broke into sobs;
   But Nicholas called, not loudly, but the way he had,
   " In olden times a children's army marched
   Across the sea dry-shod; and they, indeed,
   Were children but of one named Israel,
   While we are Christ's!
   The sea will hedge itself on either side
   And leave a path for us to walk between."
   So we believed and sang beneath the stars.
   The next day, verily, we saw the sea
   And Genoa, beneath whose walls we camped.
   Nicholas named the following dawn as hour

When we should march dry-shod across the sea.
How happy we who had been faithful to the end!
Our labors all were done. We could not sleep.
Long before dawn I went to Nicholas
And knelt and begged that I might be
Among the first of them that walked into the sea.
He flung his arms around me and cried out,
" David, we two shall lead the lambs of God."
After a long, long time the dawn began:
The army knelt and prayed together the last time,
And rose, and with their flowers and their roods
Marched solemnly unto the water's edge;
And first of all went Nicholas and I.
The water touched my shoes and did not part;
But yet I knew it would and kept right on.
Deeper and deeper — my knees — my waist — the cold
Stole to my heart — the prayers died out within me.
But I kept on. And I was blind before
The water reached my eyes and smothered me.

GUIDO. And then?
DAVID. I lay on the beach in the sun,
    People laughing and shouting around . . .
GUIDO. That was the end?
DAVID. The end. The lambs were scattered.
    In time they hid themselves about the world.
GUIDO. And you?
DAVID. A little band that still could not believe
    God would so fool and trap them, went to Rome
    To tell Christ's shepherd there, the Pope.
    I went along, not knowing where to go.
GUIDO. The Holy Father said?

DAVID.   That we were disobedient, pert children,
    That we should go with speed back to our homes,
    That we might win forgiveness if, when grown,
    We took the sword to win Christ's Sepulchre.
    So I knew that the world was bad, and one
    Must live in it awhile like any beast.
    I stole away, came here, and — here I am.
    That is my life!
    You say the world is beautiful, the spring
    Is God's, that road is lately trod by Christ —
    Lies! lies! God is not here! I don't believe!

(*It has grown dusk. The old man suddenly rises and strides forward to
    DAVID. He seems tall and fearful; his voice is terrible.*)

SERLE DE LANLARAZON.   He is! Thou *dost* believe! Naught else so
        plain!
    Dost think this marvelous, shining soul of thine,
    That will not shatter into common vileness,
    Though tested with the blows of agony,
    Can be a cup for aught but heavenly wine?
    Lo, thou dost brim with God!
GUIDO.   Who art thou, strange and terrible old man?
SERLE.   Serle de Lanlarazon, the heretic!
    I, too, was once a soldier of the Lord,
    O shepherd boy, and I, too, met defeat.
    They that were noblest of the sons of men
    I have seen butchered, and the land of all
    Lands peacefulest ravished and soaked in blood!
    Mine eyes beheld five hundred women burned
    At Carcassonne — they walked into the flames
    As into lovers' arms! When Béziers fell,

> They that were burned, women and boys and babes,
> Escaped such tortures and abominations
> As made the flames seem tenderer than sleep.
> Yet, blinded by injustice too clear seen,
> Shall I denial make of Him that steels
> This vile and coward soul of ours
> To unendurable and gainless agonies?
> Yea, verily, His acts, seen singly, take
> The cast of madness, and but momently
> We see what is as wisdom. Yet behold,
> Nothing can goad the bleeding soul of man
> Unto sublimity that tops the stars,
> Like undeservèd wrong and mad injustice!
> These women that died horribly for faith,
> Your children urged to folly by a dream,
> The broken spirits of the world that are
> Its torches — these are the testament of fire
> Struck from the flint! What hand but His
> Could draw from this poor stuff of ours — Light!
> Who sees the flame hath seen divinity!

GUIDO. What was the evil that your people wrought
> There in Provence to earn such punishment?

SERLE. They saw the truth and dared to speak it loud!
> Against them stood the Church of Rome, once pure,
> But now become as foul as leprosy!

> (DAVID *and* GUIDO *are horrified.*)

> We fearlessly cried out, " Unclean, unclean!
> Beseech the healing hands of Christ, proud Rome."

GUIDO (*aside to* DAVID). He does not know!

SERLE. But she that called herself the church of Christ,
> Hearing the truth, slew them that dared to speak.

GUIDO.   What need was there to speak? In Sicily,
　　　We see her faults, as you, but let them be.
SERLE.   Then ye are cowards!
　　　My people have a more heroic heart.
　　　Wilt call it life to see the truth struck down
　　　And not unsheathe thy sword in her defense?
　　　Wilt call it life to hear the voice of God
　　　But cravenly to hide and mute the tidings?
　　　Life, life —
　　　Is't not the test of all we know as good
　　　Embattled 'gainst the all we know as evil,
　　　The Eternal Right against the Eternal Wrong?
　　　O child, the perfume and the bloom of life,
　　　Youth's song of yearning underneath the moon,
　　　These fade. But there's a splendor never fades;
　　　And he enlisting as God's knight-at-arms
　　　Wages a fight that has not any end,
　　　Whose prize more sacred is than Palestine,
　　　Whose gain's no tomb, but an eternal life.
DAVID.   Then thou'dst not counsel us to cross the sea
　　　And go crusading to Jerusalem?
SERLE.   His fight is not across the seas, but here!
GUIDO.   Then were the battles that my heroes fought —
　　　Richard and Godfrey and the rest — all wrong?
SERLE.   Nay, nay. Somehow, it is God's deep desire
　　　That stirs the hearts of men to that adventure.
　　　But 'tis a fool's adventure! To you, to me,
　　　How could His Tomb more potent be to save
　　　Than any field of earth where flowers grow?
　　　The noble striving's everything, and Christ
　　　In kindness let them fail! . . .

Yet, fairer far the quest for that poor Tomb
Than all the wars that men have waged before
For hate or gain or merely idleness. . . .
The world grows better. . . . Thou sayest Simon's dead?

DAVID.   Ay.

SERLE.   And Innocent that preached the war?

DAVID.   Dead, too.

SERLE.   And there is peace 'twixt heretic and Church?

DAVID.   The wars have ceased.

GUIDO.   And there's for emperor
A friend of truth, no matter how bedight —
A host to all the wisdom of the world
Though hailing from Provence or India.
Arab and Jew, Mohammedan and Greek,
Find courtesy and hearing in Palermo.

SERLE.   Have I not heard the coming of the Lord?
The darkness giveth forth much inner light
And loneliness lets in diviner guests.
The years of my captivity have brought
Much wisdom I had missed. Even, I trace
Nobility in them that tortured us!
Simon and Innocent worked for a God
That is my God, although their work was mad
And evil only. We who swore that Evil was
Itself eternal and not born of Good,
Who died for that belief, we were not wholly wise.
It is a truth, but one forgetting which
Need vary not one whit the lives of men.
All know that good and evil are at war,
And in that war all lordly souls enlist,

Roman or heretic or infidel.
What matter the first cause? For battle-cry
To all the gallantry beneath the stars,
Two words suffice: " He is! " . . .
I long for but one thing before I die —
Not to incite my people 'gainst the Pope,
Nor bear the southern standard in the strife,
But to assure them of the living God. . . .
Across the edges of the world there blows a wind
Mysterious with perfume of a spring;
A spring that is not of the kindling earth,
That's more than scent of bloom or gleam of bud;
The spring of God in flower!
Down there where neither sun nor air came through,
I felt it blow across my dungeon walls —
The wind before the footsteps of the Lord!
It bloweth now across the world;
It strangely stirs the hearts of men; wars cease;
Rare deeds familiar grow; fastings and prayers,
Forgiveness, poverty; temples are built
On visioned impulses, and children march
On journeys with no end.
Far off, far off He comes,
And we are swept upon our knees
As meadow grasses kneeling to the wind.
GUIDO.   Thou man of God!

(He falls impetuously on his knees before SERLE, *catching hold of his hands. So close, he sees his hideous, disfigured face and falls back with an involuntary cry of loathing. It is twilight.)*

SERLE (*gazing intently at his hands*). Are these my hands? Rotted and numb!

(*He slowly realizes, and with a strangled groan falls to the ground.*)

SERLE. Leper! Leper!
GUIDO. Old man, old man, forgive me!
DAVID. Hush . . . He speaks!
SERLE. Dost think that I have lived these bloody years,
    Endured these agonies and fought this fight,
    That I should now deliver thee my soul
    Because thou eatest away this flesh of mine,
    Stealing the maggots' certain meal? Back, back,
    O Prince of Darkness, this flame thou canst not eat!

(*Staggers to his feet.*)

    Shepherd, I feel the stars!
DAVID. There will be many soon.
SERLE (*lifting his arms*). God of battles, I, that was a man,
    Do offer up to Thee that which remains!
    Thine enemy hath eat the flesh of me
    And made me fetid in the sight of men,
    And soon he sendeth death to bear me hence.
    O Lord, the little life vouchsafèd me,
    Let it not waste in useless burial.
    Thou comest soon again to see Thy people.
    O let me go once more to my Provence
    To tell them of Thy coming and of Thee!
    Thou that dost love the fighting heart of man,
    Let me prepare them! Let me, O Lord, go home.
DAVID (*kneeling*). Lord, I am Thy child! Forgive me all
    And let me fight again in Thy behalf!
    Bless me, old man, for I shall take thee home.

GUIDO. David, thou'lt set him free?
DAVID. And more, much more.
  I'll go with him, protect him, follow him,
  And preach with him the God he's shown to me. . . .
  I'll steal the horses and set forth to-night;
  Across the Tuscan border we are safe.
GUIDO. But what, old man, is this that you would preach?
SERLE. Prepare, prepare! The Lord walks in His world!
GUIDO. And should they ask your name?
SERLE. Serle de Lanlarazon.
GUIDO. The heretic!
SERLE. But come to preach with late-learned gentleness
  A God all men accept.
DAVID. The wars have ceased, Guido.
GUIDO. Because the heretics are slain.
SERLE. They could not wholly die.
GUIDO. If they should ask, " Serle de Lanlarazon,
  When you cursed Rome, did you then lie? "
SERLE. It was the truth.
GUIDO. Is evil still itself, eternal?
SERLE. As always, hence the eternal strife.
GUIDO. Do you recant? Submit you to the church?
SERLE. A thousand times, no.
GUIDO. David, you ride to death!
  When they discover he who preaches God's
  Lanlarazon, they'll burn the two of you,
  No matter if his words were learned of Christ!
SERLE. Wouldst counsel cowardice?
GUIDO. Not that, I swear, not that! But what's the gain?
SERLE. There is no gain, perhaps; the fight is all.
GUIDO. I see no fight. I see a wide-flung glory,

  A world that is not bad, so full of beauty

  I need no proof, as thou, it comes from God.

Serle. The beauty thou dost know is temporal.

  Thou seest the world dew-drenched! 'Tis drenched in **blood**!

Guido. I am not less a-shine with God than thou!

Serle. The God of youth, a fair god but most frail.

Guido. Him I adore; I see, I need no other.

Serle. Already thou dost fear and wait His death!

  This little prelude to eternity,

  Is it an hour of roses and of song?

  This throe that leads at last to heaven or hell,

  Is loveliness its only quality?

  What of the large endurance of the soul?

  The heroic heart, the wild nobility?

Guido. All that will come — I have so many years to live!

Serle. If thou wert free this instant, where wouldst thou go?

Guido. To Sicily!

Serle. Once there, what wouldst thou do?

Guido. The Emperor's court has thousands of delights.

Serle. And is that all?

Guido. Then, later —

Serle. What? What?

David. No crusades, Guido.

Serle. Wilt thou not offer up thy gallant heart

  To something sterner than delights of youth?

  Thou hast drunk deep of happiness, wilt still

  Drink on, oblivious to all but bliss?

  (*Tenderly.*) Child of the springtime voice, could youth last always

  There were no need of heaven. . . .

  In youth the world is but an April wood

  Through which we ride with holiday, light hearts.

The boughs are dreamy with new-opened blooms,
The laughter of the air shakes petals down,
The forest paths are dappled with the sun,
And youth rides by with half-closed, taunting eyes,
Drinking his fill of Life's delicious prime,
In idleness that is a noble dream.
He hears the breathing of the magic world,
And, head-bent, listens to the inner song
That gushes lustrously from his own heart.
Yet, as he rides, anon he hears far off
Across the boughs a trumpet note; he stops,
And something stirs and answers deep in him.
The sound fades; on he rides. A nearer blast
Shouts out; Youth listens with his lifted eyes;
Another! The blossoms are broken! Another, more loud!
And suddenly all of the wood is shaken with trumpets and shouts
And calls and commands and sounds of the battle affray.
For, lo! the wood leads out to the bloody, bare plain
Where the legions of God are engaged to the death.
Hard pressed are the knights of the Lord; they charge and are felled,
And arise and return to be slain.
And over the clamor and dust of the fight,
The thundering voice of the Lord
Giving heart to the banners of purple and red of His hosts!
And filled with the dreams and the wonder he learned in the woods,
Youth rushes in, turns his back to the sunshine and glamor,
Draws sword and brings succor to them that are faint
And oppressed with the strife, and fights on till he dies.
Thou too, thou too art lordly-souled, O youth,

Thou wilt not shun the sword-play of thy God!
Choose! The bare plain is ahead!

DAVID (*turning passionately to* GUIDO).   Come with us, Guido. His
    words seem God's to me;
And thou art not afraid. Thou broughtest
Into the evil world around me here
Goodness, and I remembered Nicholas.
Thou art my only friend. Come with us, Guido.

(GUIDO *stands with lifted head, deeply moved, uncertain. A film of
    amethyst afterglow is across the west; there are many stars. Intense
    silence, then the sound of a shepherd's flute rises from the road,
    passes, and fades. A long pause.* GUIDO *listens, entranced.*)

GUIDO.   Didst hear that flute?
SERLE.   Not when the voice of God rings in my ears!
GUIDO (*passionately*).   My God spoke also! My God is not your God!
    Why do ye think the trees disrobe themselves
In gales of color gorgeously,
Instead of one swift greyness;
Why do ye think the stars swing past
In visible magnificence?
The sea could bear its traffic
Without the tumult of its coloring;
Sheep could be led without that shepherd's fluting,
And children born without the primrose moon
In western skies! Deaf and blind!
Ye speak as transients through life, who know
Nothing of this divine, mysterious earth
My element! Speak not to me of purposes,
Sure death, eternal wrong!
I am a leaf of scarlet,

A summer-tinted cloud,
A kiss in the dark, forgotten soon,
But red, desired of many!
Hell does not gape beneath my feet, and if
About my head the almond blossoms crowd,
What need have I of heaven? . . . David, David,
I cannot go!

(*A pause. The sound of horses approaching on the road. All listen.*)

GUIDO. The guards returning!
DAVID. No, not before midnight.
GUIDO. What can it be? . . . God, let me out of this place!
(*The horses stop below. A boy's voice calls " Master! "*)
GUIDO (*calls down*). Felice! It's my page, David! He's come for me!
Page of mine, come up, come quickly up!
(*Watching over the parapet.*)
An empty saddle! That's for me! Free, free!
They've tied their horses just below us —
They've crossed the moat — They're coming —
Sicily! At last! At last!
DAVID (*rousing himself*). But you are prisoners!
If you are seen, then I am prisoner too.
(*Sound of footsteps in the corridor.*) Too late!

(FELICE, *a thirteen-year-old page, rushes in, leaps into* GUIDO's *arms.
A guard follows with a torch; fixes it in the wall and goes out.*)

FELICE. Master, I found the Emperor at Capua
In conference with the papal delegates.
The long feud's at an end.
He and the Pope are friends and you're released —
Downstairs his nuncio makes all arrangements.
Our horses wait below!

GUIDO. What a page! David, you know Felice.
   I wish that you could go with us!
   We'll start at once. Good-bye, good-bye,
   Dear friends, we're off to Sicily!
FELICE. Not Sicily.
GUIDO. Not Sicily?
FELICE. The Emperor sends us on a mission north.
GUIDO. But where?
FELICE. Into Provence.
GUIDO. With roundelays to some fair Queen of Love?
FELICE. Nay, Master, 'tis at last the great adventure!
GUIDO. Speak out, Felice.
FELICE. We bear the tidings of a great crusade.
   To-morrow we'll be soldiers of the Cross.
GUIDO. Go on.
FELICE. The Pope has won the Emperor's consent
   To lead an army 'gainst the heretics.
GUIDO. 'Tis a lie!
FELICE. It is the truth.
   And we to bishops, princes, potentates
   Bring the good news —
   War, war, till the last heretic is dead.
SERLE. My people, O my people!
   Shepherd, we must go now!
DAVID. Too late. The guard who brought the page is now below
   Warning them I've unloosed the prisoners.
   They will return to put us both in chains.
SERLE. O God, the murders and the burnings once again!
   Must the truth die utterly, utterly!

(A sound of footsteps.)

DAVID. There is the guard.

GUIDO. Close that door. (DAVID *hesitates*.) Close it,
Bolt it.

(DAVID *and* FELICE *close and bolt the great door leading into the interior of the castle.*)

GUIDO. Up on my shoulder, page. Take down the ladder.

(FELICE *on* GUIDO'S *shoulder climbs up and takes down the rope ladder from* GUIDO'S *window.*)

'Twill reach the ground.

(*A loud knock on the door.*)

Quick, make it fast.

(*They fasten the ladder to the parapet so that it drops to the road. Voices inside call "Open!"*)

GUIDO (*calls out*). I am the prisoner to be released.
Three minutes, friends, while I change raiment. . . .
David, Felice, take the old man down,
Ride north!
Five minutes' start and you are safe.
Go, warn them that so soon must die.

DAVID. But you?

GUIDO (*taking* DAVID'S *broadsword*). I'll hold them here.

FELICE. Master —

GUIDO. Go, page of mine, Felice.

SERLE. Thou child of God!

(DAVID *falls on his knees and catches* GUIDO'S *hand, overcome.*)

GUIDO. Go, David, quickly, quickly — God-speed!

(FELICE *and* DAVID *with difficulty help* SERLE *over the parapet and disappear.* GUIDO *stands before the door, leaning on his sword.*)

How hatefully thou lovest me, God!

Voices within. Open.

GUIDO. Another minute, friends!

(*Cries of " Open," confused noise; they batter on the door, finally breaking it in.*)

GUIDO. Back, there, villains!

(GUIDO *rushes in with the broadsword, forcing them into the passageway. The sound of horses' hoofs; it dies out.* GUIDO *fights desperately; a guard rushes under his arm, stabs him. He staggers and falls. The guards enter, look around, think he is dead and go out. Enter* FELICE *over the edge of the parapet.*)

FELICE. Master Master!

(*Finds* GUIDO *and lifts him in his arms.*)

GUIDO. Thou, Felice? . . . Thou didst return to me?

FELICE. I could not leave thee.

GUIDO. I'm glad. . . . And they have gone?

FELICE. They're safe. . . . But thou art wounded!

GUIDO. I'm glad we are alone. 'Tis almost like

Dying in Sicily.

FELICE. Master, thou canst not die!

GUIDO. I should not die.

Death has mistook his quarry, and Jesus sleeps.

(*He sinks down.*)

FELICE (*terrified*). I'll fetch a priest.

GUIDO. Stay here.

I am beyond the laying on of hands.

My deeds were not. My aspirations lacked

Not beauty, but singleness of purpose.

And I have lived.

No priest can mend what's broken here.

And for the rest . . .
Persephone or Mary will recall
That I on earth was young and beautiful. . . .
Help me up, page, where I may see the world.
>(FELICE *supports him to the parapet.*)
I shall miss the iris skies and wet, clear stars
Of these our April evenings . . .
And thee, Felice . . .
Can any other world be half so lovely,
Or any other life so sweet?
This earthly ecstasy not yet half-lived,
This heady vintage of days and nights
Sipped only . . . Perhaps it is as well. . . .
When thou dost see Palermo, rising from the sea,
Felice, think of me. . . .
The bursting wave of life,
Breast it with twofold joy, remembering me.

FELICE (*sobbing*). I am thy page. Ah, leave me not alone.

GUIDO. Hush, hush! But yet, forget me never.
Hold me — I cannot see — There, there —
I would that now I could find words of counsel
Which might protect thee always; but
I, too, am young and still untaught.
Yet treasure this:
Pray often, as you sing, unthinkingly;
'Twill Jesus please, and then, it sweetens one.
O littlest comrade of my heart,
Doubt not the world is good and mankind mostly noble.
That I have lived unstained
Hath profited me surely by the gift
Of deep delight. The lips of harlotry

  Can never kiss the sun
  With the light rapture that was ours. . . .
  The rest I did not learn.
FELICE. Why didst thou fight to save those men, Master?
GUIDO. Something about God — I can't remember —
  I *had* to fight —
  Closer, Felice. . . . I'm sleepy.
  Sing me that song we made
  As we rode up from Sicily.
FELICE. I cannot.
GUIDO. The little song . . .
FELICE (*sings*).

     Jesu,
    If Thou wilt make
    Thy peach trees bloom for me,
    And fringe my bridle paths both sides
    With tulips red and free,
    If Thou wilt make Thy skies as blue
      As ours in Sicily,
    And wake the little leaves that sleep
      On every bending tree,
    I promise not to vexen Thee
    That Thou shouldst make eternally
      Heaven, my home.
     But right contentedly —

Master! Master!
                (*Guido dies.*)
Voice of the Madman. Son of David, have mercy on us!

NEW MOON

                    Now day,
Drawing his golden waters down the west,
Forsakes the loitering, low-bosomed moon.
Naked amid the unaccustomed stars
She stands, afraid, then down the shining ebb
Hastens to hide her girlish loveliness
From their too youthful wonder in the sea.

WHERE ILIUM WAS PROUD

Along the sands where Ilium was proud
A crimson laurel bush, that draws, perhaps,
From Priam's ancient buried house its blood,
Sprinkles with flame the unbeholding waste
In luxury of summer-hearted bliss.
Ah, better so its given years to burn
Unseen of maidens and young warriors
Than, plucked untimely, to have flushed an hour
The white of Helen's bosom on a night
When Paris leaned across the lights and laughter
To drink her up with hot, unmanly eyes.
Its crimson, fading with the dawn, had been
Only a deathless tale in poets' mouths.

EURIPIDES

To him the fate we bear was like a sea
That sweeps above the many ships that sailed,
And waits as home for all that sail again.
Bitter intolerably, and deep as death;
But shining, too, shining and full of spray,
In color stainèd lovelier than the sky,
Singing a requiem for them that die
Adventuring on its bounds, or, dauntless, sing
When roaring and inevitable wash
Heaves down the prows. . . . His heart was full of stars,
His prayers only to gods that deathlessly
Abide and dream no sin. And Syracuse
That builded on the sea, loved his name most.

FAREWELL TO ETNA

Great mountain, swathed in blue with foamy crest
Of fire, majestic as the mighty sea,
Thy brother and immortal comrade close,
The stars except, sole comrade fitting, equal —
Only, perhaps, as dust upon the wind
Shall I behold again thy spreading might.
Yet no regret is mine. I have thee in
My soul, though lodgment base, where room the stars
And many a tide of vestal-footed ocean.
Nor waste I tears that now the Cyclops brood
Is dead, and never hoarse, heroic blast
Shall hurl again in white and purple yeast
Odysseus and the dark-eyed mariners.
Nor foe of gods nor friend thy splendor saw
Than now more dark, more high majestical.
Thy color of solemnity doth stain
The temporal and wayward thing I house.
But if, when I am sown upon the air,
Another, seeing thee against the sunken sun
In folds of wine-dark gauze and amethyst,
Should rise to exaltation more superb
Than mine, and praise with loftier flight of soul
Thy splendor that to-night is all my own —
That were regret! Lend me thy purple thought,
Eternal brooding vigilant, that I
May counsel with my soul to rival his.

THE IMMORTAL RESIDUE

Love and the lofty heart and tears — these three
Immortal are, and draw eternally
Deep from the young world's loveliness their life.
The kiss, the prayer, the cry — the same to-day
As when the brute with noble pang distressed
Cleared the abysm and was man. Than these
Not surer come the stars, nor flooding up
The rainy slopes of spring dark violets.
More utterly than sunset cloud dissolved,
Soft Syracuse has passed. The bannered fleet
That flashed into her harbor scornfully
Left not a ghostly sail to haunt the blue.
And they that heard in Athens ere they came
Great Socrates, whose spoken word was like
The calm intoning of the lustral ocean,
Before they perished in their slavery,
Bequeathed not any dream for us to learn.
Nor shall we know the thought of those tall girls
That stood where now the yellow gorse stands high,
And in their golden, fluttering loveliness
Watched the young prisoners. Instead, remain
The bay, the bubble air, the secret dust,
These, and the mortal kinship that we own.
Kisses they whispered for I beg to-day.
Their eyes did never blur but I could guess.
And as their spirits stood, tall as the sword
Of one that guards the portal of a queen

And leans thereon in moonlight, mine hath stood.
I know their loves and wingèd hearts and tears,
And mine shall every man that lives know too;
And so the same, forever, to the close.
Perhaps some spring a thousand years from now
Two crowned ineffably with youth, their hearts
A-toss in wind-flower dance before the sun,
Loitering lover-wise across the fields
And empty places that I knew, may chance
Upon the rubble where I dream, and muse:
" Those old barbarians, dead so long ago,
Was life to them so fair, and did the sun
Shine honey-sweet into their open hearts?
Could they have ever dreamed such love as ours,
Or dared, O love, this slow, divinest kiss?"
Their words, I know, shall warm the flower roots
That were my heart. To them as now to me
May day be only blue; all moon the night;
And may enamored fate a little while
Hold back their portion due of tears and dark.

SET OF MOON

The archeress had gone;
A western hill across her path still bore
The magic of her recent footing there;
And upwards all the air was lustral pure.
The city slept, but far above shone bright
The city of the gods that never sleep.

PART II

IN APRIL ONCE, AND OTHER POEMS

II

LYRICAL PIECES

OVERTONES

I heard a bird at break of day
    Sing from the autumn trees
A song so mystical and calm,
    So full of certainties,
No man, I think, could listen long
    Except upon his knees.
Yet this was but a simple bird
    Alone, among dead trees.

IN NEW YORK

1. ON SUNDAY MORNING

Far, far from here the church bells ring,
    As when I was a child,
And there is one I dearly love
    Walks in the sunlight mild.
To church she goes, and with her once
    I went, a little child.

The church bells ring far, far away,
    The village streets are bright,
The sunlight falls in slanting bars
    And fills the church with light.
And I remember when I knelt
    Beside her, in delight.

There's something lost, there's something lost,
    Some wisdom has beguiled!
My heart has flown a thousand miles
    And in the sunlight mild
I kneel and weep beside her there
    As she prays for her child.

2. THE SONG YOU LOVE

When I have sung the sweet songs and the sad,
The songs of magic drifting from above,
The trumpet songs that shout across men's souls,

The sleep-song, breasted softer than the dove,
Still there will be one song I have not sung —
  The song you love, the song you love.

What are the torches of the world to you,
The words that comfort men and calm their fears?
What are the stars with their strange harmonies,
Or fate that shadows all, or death that jeers?
There must be laughter in the song you love
  And at the end there must be tears.

When I have come to that green place we know
Where cedars stand that have no faith in spring,
Where through the utter peace of afternoon
The mocking-birds their heartless raptures fling,
Long after it is dust, one heart there'll be
  Restless with words it could not sing.

3. WEARINESS

I sometimes think Thou art my secret love;
But not to-night. . . . To-night I have the need
Of human tenderness; not hovering wings,
But one warm breast where I may lay my head
And close my eyes. For I am tired to-night. . . .
The park was full of lovers,
And such a slender moon looked down on them. . . .
For one kiss of one mouth, free-given, I
Would give — what's left of me to-night
To the last dream!
Art Thou a jealous god?
Dost think to force by loneliness

Unwilling love to Thee?
Beware, beware! The winds of madness blow
Strong, strong on nights like these! . . .
Thou dost deny me what's of life most sweet,
The bending head and lovely eyes of love —
Then give, beseech Thee, give me sleep.

4. IN THE NIGHT

Drifting, groping
For delight;
Longing, hoping
All the night.
Perfume of
Blossomed hair —
Where is love?
Ah, no, not there! . . .
Not there.

Turning, turning,
Sleepless-eyed,
Something burning
At my side —
Winds that sweep
Poppied hair,
Where is sleep?
Ah, no, not there! . . .
Not there?

5. HOME

I have a need of silence and of stars;
Too much is said too loudly; I am dazed.

The silken sound of whirled infinity
Is lost in voices shouting to be heard.
I once knew men as earnest and less shrill.
An undermeaning that I caught I miss
Among these ears that hear all sounds save silence,
These eyes that see so much but not the sky,
These minds that gain all knowledge but no calm.
If suddenly the desperate music ceased,
Could they return to life? or would they stand
In dancers' attitudes, puzzled, polite,
And striking vaguely hand on tired hand
For an encore, to fill the ghastly pause?
I do not know. Some rhythm there may be
I cannot hear. But I — oh, I must go
Back where the breakers of deep sunlight roll
Across flat fields that love and touch the sky;
Back to the more of earth, the less of man,
Where there is still a plain simplicity,
And friendship, poor in everything but love,
And faith, unwise, unquestioned, but a star.
Soon now the peace of summer will be there
With cloudy fire of myrtles in full bloom;
And, when the marvelous wide evenings come,
Across the molten river one can see
The misty willow-green of Arcady.
And then — the summer stars . . . I will go home.

THE WANDERER

I have grown weary of the open sea,
The chartless ways, the storms, the loneliness,
The coast that topples, tall and shelterless —
Weary of faring where all things are free!

Yet once the open sea was all romance,
Purple and olive-stained and golden-scaled;
And every breeze from some adventure hailed,
And shoals were silver for the moon to dance.

The cliffs were only tall to keep untrod
The kingdom of the fay hung high in air,
And every storm was but Poseidon's dare,
And brave it was to battle with a god.

Ah, blithe it was when the mad night was done
And day with flying hair woke wild and white,
To see the salty sail loom in the light
And know one battle more was bravely won.

Then these were magic seas that ever rang
With melodies, now wild, now sweet, now glad;
At dusk the drifting choirs unseen were sad
And in the lulls of night the sirens sang.

They sing no more; the colors now are grey;
The cliffs defend not fairyland, but home;

And when th' impenitent, hoar sea has clomb
The clouds, I have no heart to sing or pray.

Oh, I am weary of the open sea,
Vigils and storms and watches without name,
The ache of long resistance without aim,
The fetters of the fetterless and free.

There is some haven that no tempest mars,
Some brown-hilled harbor, hushed and clear and deep,
Where tired evening may sit down and weep,
And, waking, find not water there but stars.

There would I creep at last ere day is done,
With ashen sail dropped down and cordage white;
There rest secure, there find before the night
A little hour of peace, a little sun!

THE MAN IN WHITE

(Ambulance drivers from the Front tell that to the grievously wounded, alone on the battlefield, the hallucination often comes of a man in white who comforts them.)

   " Soldier, knowest thou the land
    The land that's home to thee? "
   " Stranger, with the voice not strange,
    Why do you lean to me,
   A wounded man, and put a word
    That mocks my memory? "

   " Soldier, I am from that land,
    The land that's home to thee."
   " O stranger with the gentle hands,
    Now let your pity be.
   You have no word what land is mine,
    Your closed eyes cannot see
   As mine, as mine, the land of lands,
    The land where I would be."

   " I see a field of apple trees
    That top a furrowed hill,
   A little house, a little room,
    A flowered window sill.
   A woman with a face like thine,
    But eyes more sweet and still,
   Who prays across the gathered dusk
    To guard her child from ill."

"My God, my God, I fear to look
    Lest there be no man by!
If this be but a fever dream
    O let me sleep and die
And never know a blessed ghost
    From home had heard my cry."

"See me, touch me, let thy head
    On my bosom weigh.
This, the kiss your mother sent,
    That on your lips I lay."
"Yes — it is hers — no other drives
    The awful pain away —
I think — that I could fall asleep —
    If you — would only — stay."

"Rest thee, rest thee on my breast,
    Let the deep sleep come.
Rest thee, rest thee, soldier lad,
    Time is past to roam.
Waking, I shall still be near,
    And we shall be at home."

THE WOOD

There was a knight once rode from out the sun
Into a twilight wood, forever still.
It was a place for blue-eyed knights to shun,
For such are liefer to enchantments ill.
Deep in the wood he rode with head bent low . . .
There was no sound save tired leaves that fell.
His lance hung listless from his saddle bow;
Pale was his armor; pale his mouth as well.
The old adventures and the knightly bouts
Seemed faint and far as shapes in fever seen.
Because his dreams had died, but not his doubts,
His eyes were grey that had been blue, I ween.

But whether he that haunted wood passed through,
Or came unto the marsh, I never knew.

IN THE STORM

The shining moments are so far between!
From their clear crests we see the dawn unfurled
In films of opal on the dew-drenched world —
Life, life, dædal, harmonious, serene!
Then darkness. For that aërial wide scene,
Tempests down mountain by-paths madly hurled;
This way and that our tortured souls are whirled,
Blinded, aghast, beneath the lightning's green.
The peaks are moments; lifelong lasts the dark.
Yet, soul, be strong! Thou hast beheld the sun,
Hast known that life is wisdom and is one.
Stanch thy despair! The cloud-rack thou dost mark
May hide a crest whereto thy wanderings bend.
And this, too, ends. There is a certain end.

MR. W. H. TO THE POET

(THANKING HIM FOR A COPY OF "THE TEMPEST")

My thanks, dear friend, as always! But, I fear
No art — not Prospero's — can speak to me
As those swift words you breathed first in my ear.
They were your heart; this but your wizardry.
We have lived much, won much, and now are old.
Strange, is it not, when I call in review
My life's achievements, dross and drab and gold,
There's nothing shines but took its light from you?
And yet, as I reread our book to-night,
And trembled almost at some old-loved line,
I wondered if the world, so prone to slight,
Would some day slur your stainless name with mine,
Not knowing there is ice in heavenly flame,
And Friendship is Love's canonizèd name.

NOVEMBER

How has November won
    More loveliness
With opal mist and sun
    Than spring can boast?

The village houses all
    Wear aureoles.
Their smoke is pale and tall
    As Abel's was.

The winds adoringly
    On tiptoe pause,
Nor grudge the branches free
    Slow gift of leaves.

And on the air one note
    Clear, clear, and sad,
From the unmated throat
    Of some lone bird.

O earth, that doth confess
    In beauty God,
How calm the happiness,
    How close the tears!

PROLOGUE

Whose blood runs gay as summer's,
Whose heart is sure and proud,
Whose days are all newcomers,
Whose nights are dream-endowed, —
Pass on, lest you should hear
Speech neither sweet nor clear.

Whose blood is slowly spilling,
Whose heart has crimson scars,
Whose days have lost their thrilling,
Whose nights have lost their stars —
Pause here and you will find
One of your kith and kind.

TO AN OLD TUNE

You cannot choose but love, lad,
From dawn till twilight dreary;
You cannot choose but love, lad,
Though love grows weary, weary.

For, lad, an if you love not,
You'd best have slept, unwaking;
But, O, an if you love, lad,
Your heart is breaking, breaking.

Though friends and lovers only
Fill life with joyous breath,
Yet friend or lover only
Can make you pray for death.

Throw open wide your heart then,
Love's road-house for a mile!
And if one turns to leave you
Or stab you — smile, lad, smile.

A HUNGER SONG

Some are fed on kingly fare,
    Some starve, as fate decrees;
Of those death takes away the soul,
    The body takes of these.

I would not have my soul to die;
    Too soon corruption comes.
But two deaths I had rather die,
    Than live and live on crumbs.

There is a banquet table set
    Within a silver gate
Where lads and maidens lightly feast —
    Outside the beggars wait.

Oh, starve me, food and drink denied,
    Or gorge till soul succumbs,
But I'll not live as beggars do —
    Feed me not, Love, on crumbs.

DEFEAT

Though you have struck me to the bloody core,
It is indeed only one scar the more!
And I'll not turn from you as at the other strokes,
Nor say " Good-bye," as other times I said.
    The agony still chokes,
And still it seems most restful to be dead.
But I'll not say " Good-bye " nor turn away,
    Nor parting lover play. . . .
Leave you? Take everything save all — my heart?
I know the scene too well, too well my part!
Hot tears and bitterness; and I would go,
Go for an hour, a day, a week —
Is bitterness so short called pique?
And in the old, old way, without regret
    I would return to you;
And in the old, old way you would forget
    That ever I had gone, and let
        Some casual tenderness
        Be my return's caress;
Or in some vague, absorbed distress,
Lift up your shadow eyes to mine still wet.

LULLABY

Sleep, brown-eyed, sleep.
'Tis but the winds that weep,
Telling from tree to tree
Their ancient misery.
'Tis but the winds that weep.
    Sleep. . . . Sleep.
'Tis but the touch of dreams
Upon your mouth that seems
Like groping kisses . . . Sleep!
    'Tis but the dreams . . .
And, oh, 'tis but the dew
So bitter tastes to you,
Falling the long night through,
Falling on lips untrue —
    The dew, only the dew.

SANCTUARY

Sweep over me, O lovely winds,
    That shake the tasseled oak!
The patience of the ancient earth
    Turns blossom at your stroke,
The very grievance of the air
    Thins out to silver smoke.

Sweep over me, O youthful winds,
    And I will lie as dead
Upon the leaves that lived last year,
    With new leaves overhead.
Has your beneficence no balm
    For hearts grown wearièd?

There's weariness of labor done
    That dark and sleep appease;
And fragrant weariness of flesh,
    Delightfuller than ease;
But there's a weariness that comes
    More wearily than these,

With neither blossoms in its hair,
    Nor sleepy sound of rain,
Nor bearing ointments to allay
    The heart that's sick with pain.
There is a weariness that comes
    And does not go again.

O ancient earth that never tires,
    O heavens that renew,
O winds that foam and flash and blow
    Forever fresh as dew,
There is a wounded thing that lies
    Face down, and calls on you.

AUTUMNAL

To-night the tumult of the autumn wind
Rushes between the ragged grey of heaven
And earth's autumnal grey — swift, swift and loud —
Filled with the wings of wild birds southward blown
And with the wings of leaves that only fly
Their red and golden flight when they are dead.
And we who keep unwillingly the earth,
Are caught, are caught up with the birds and the leaves,
Are whirled above the spare, unblossoming fields,
Along the pallid torrents of the air,
Far from the earth we know, past the dead moon,
Beyond the blue-lit, scattered spheres of night
That flicker down the dark like shaken leaves,
On, on, with the rushing wind of autumn,
Out to the stark, last outpost of creation
Where nothingness surges. . . .
From that wan strand where breaks that ebon tide,
Could we behold, were spirit vision ours,
The blowing legions of the homeless dead
In wraithy phosphorus against the void?
A little while, O winds that rush and call,
A little while, O leaves, and we shall know!

A SEA BALLAD

" Is that the sea, is that the sea?
O mother dear, lean close to me.
Just there, outside the window sill,
The creeping tides are never still."
" Lie back, my son, the April breeze
Is dashing sunlight on the trees."

" I hear the sea, I hear the sea;
The breakers keen and call to me!
My father's blood was mixed with brine,
And, oh, my father's blood is mine."
" 'Tis fever makes your eyes so blue
And stains your lips with that hot hue."

" Look, look, a sail upon the sea! "
" 'Tis sunlight on the dogwood tree."
" It tacks! And now it comes straight on! "
" Merciful God, he is my son."
" Mother, I must go down to the sea! "
" Nay, son, my son, stay home with me."

" Look how they beckon, the sheet is spread."
" We are alone and I am afraid."
" They are calling me, calling me, I must go down.
They are sailing away to a strange, lonely town.
Mother, come with me. . . . Mother! . . . 'tis done."
" God without pity! O son, little son! "

AUSTRALIA IN LONDON

Between the battle over
    And the battle just begun
They give six days to wander
    And take their bit of fun
To the lads whose land lies under
    The rays of the rising sun.

No English home is theirs,
    They have no English friend —
Australia's uncivilized,
    Squatters, you know, no end!
So up they come to London
    Their bob a day to spend.

And a lad may spend it in the pubs,
    Or girls are cheap as thought —
It's not the warmth of English beer
    Or the harlot's kiss that's sought,
But those about to die have need
    Of tenderness, though bought.

Between the battle over
    And the battle not begun
They walk the streets of London,
    Strangers, frowned upon.
Yet their eyes are grey with the light
    Of the newly risen sun.

A wind from infinite skies
    Ruffles always their hair,
And the look of the birds of the sun,
    Lonely, disdainful, aware,
Is the look of their mouth and their eyes;
    They are the dreamers who dare.

They bear no arms because they must,
    They wage no conscript's war,
They fight for neither English king,
    Nor tsar nor emperor;
They heard that freedom's cause was struck,
    And freedom is their star.

Sons of the rising sun,
    With swift un-English eyes,
Not fair with white and red,
    But burnt by flaming skies,
And scornful with such youth
    As, boasting, fights and dies!

Along the Strand they swing
    With haversack and gun,
Their broad, brown hats caught up
    One side as if in fun,
And at their tunic's throat
    The sign of the rising sun.

And London furnishes,
    Though pious-eyed, askance,
Her harlots and her pubs

  To these whose very glance
Is sunlight, and who march
  To-morrow into France.

To these so infinitely young,
  So passionate to live,
That they can turn a harlot's kiss
  To love, and gladly give
What's left of them to death,
  And then have all to give.

Sons of the rising sun,
  I, from across the sea,
Drink to your gathered youth
  And your gallant chivalry.
And I would to God by your side
  We fought, as you, to be free.

December, 1916

IN OUR YARD

Moses, Moses, seeing God
    In a bush that burned,
Moses, Moses, hearing God
    Advising, unconcerned,

I believe you, for myself
    Saw Him plain and heard —
Others saw a myrtle bush
    That held a mocking-bird.

A WOOD SONG

My love is a bush in bloom,
    My love is a bird in the air,
My love is an April day,
    And a wind with golden hair.

A melody is my love
    That trembles and glistens and goes,
A forest in bud is my love
    Where hidden laughter flows.

Good-bye, O sweet-lipped maiden,
    O trusted friend, adieu!
My old love is my new love
    And dearer far than you.

THE LITTLE SHEPHERD'S SONG
(13TH CENTURY)

The leaves, the little birds, and I,
The fleece clouds and the sweet, sweet sky,
The pages singing as they ride
Down there, down there where the river is wide —
Heigh-ho, what a day! What a lovely day!
Even too lovely to hop and play
    With my sheep,
      Or sleep
    In the sun!

And so I lie in the deep, deep grass
And watch the pages as they pass,
And sing to them as they to me
Till they turn the bend by the poplar tree.
And then — O then, I sing right on
To the leaves and the lambs and myself alone!
    For I think there must be
      Inside of me
        A bird!

ADVENTURE

Who would not love to go
Out where the breakers blow,
Curling and green and slow,
    With a rose sail?
Lands there are far away,
Marvelous in the spray,
Turquoise by night, by day
    Gold as the grail.
Morning's the time to start
Just with a tipsy heart.
Wisdom a tiny part
    Taking, you fail.

TO BUTTERFLY

Do you remember how the twilight stood
And leaned above the river just to see
If still the crocus buds were in her hood
And if her robes were gold or shadowy?
Do you remember how the twilight stood
When we were lovers and the world our wood?

And then, one night, when we could find no word
But silence trembled like a heart — like mine! —
And suddenly that moon-enraptured bird
Awoke and all the darkness turned to wine?
How long ago that was! And how absurd
For us to own a wood that owned a bird!

They tell me there are magic gardens still,
And birds that sleep to wake and dream to sing,
And streams that pause for crocus skies to fill;
But they that told were lovers and 'twas spring.
Yet why the moon to-night's a daffodil
When it is March — Do you remember still?

AGRICOLÆ

I watch the farmers in their fields
    And marvel secretly.
They are so very calm and sure,
    They have such dignity.

They know such simple things so well,
    Although their learning's small,
They find a steady, brown content
    Where some find none at all.

And all their quarrellings with God
    Are soon made up again;
They grant forgiveness when He sends
    His silver, tardy rain.

Their pleasure is so grave and full
    When gathered crops are trim,
You know they think their work was done
    In partnership with Him.

Then, why, when there are fields to buy,
    And little fields to rent,
Do I still love so foolishly
    Wisdom and discontent?

RIOLAMA

(AFTER READING HUDSON'S "GREEN MANSIONS")

There is a land beyond the lands you know,
Circled by silver veils of woven rain
And green, clear sunsets with the moon in tow
And woods and dark savannahs of wild grain.

I have not wandered in the forests there,
I have not watched its willowed waters flow,
I have not breathed its leafy, upland air,
And yet, and yet, it is the land I know.

Its people's speech that my heart echoes so
To you were wild birds singing in their vine,
And other dreams and other loves they know,
But all their dreams and all their loves are mine.

They are my people! I am lost with you
And only guess the ways that I should go;
Forever homesick, baffled, yearning to
My native land that I shall never know.

A BALLAD OF ST. SEBASTIEN

1

Sebastien, Sebastien,
The archer of the King I be.
Strip off thine armor, strong and bright,
And naked stand against yon tree
For target to mine arrows' flight;
This is the King's command to thee.

O Archer, draw thy long grey bow,
Thine arrows loosen, wing by wing;
Naked I stand against the tree;
I am obedient to the King.

2

Sebastien, Sebastien,
I fit an arrow in my bow,
With poisoned laughter it is shod.
O naked knight, with head bent low,
Thus slaves bend down to take the rod —
I doubt if blood so meek can flow!

O marksman pale, with eyes of mist,
Close to my side I heard it sing!
And thou must choose a goodlier shaft
Than laughter levelled at my King.

3

Sebastien, Sebastien,
I choose me seven arrows old,
And never the heart of man they miss;
Two red, one green, two black, one gold,
And one soft-falling like a kiss.
Call up thy spirits, Knight, be bold!

Blood, blood, it flows! and oh, the kiss
Upon my heart of that warm thing!
Yet shoot another sheaf, for still
I am but wounded for my King!

4

Sebastien, Sebastien,
Behold a barb that takes away
The love of one thou lovest best.
The love it takes it does not slay,
But leaves it in another's breast. . . .
With tears the ancient barb is grey.

Oh, can it be the King ordains
This agony that slays the spring?
But for the years that thou wast loved,
Kneel down, O heart, and bless the King.

5

Sebastien, Sebastien,
Dost thou still turn thy pain to praise?
Wilt thou not die, though crimson-flecked?

Then take the shaft that never strays,
'Tis called " The Death of Self-Respect " —
Its song is laughter, and it slays.

There is no quarry left for death,
And I am dead without death's sting . . .
Take all, take all; Thou gavest all,
O Lord of mine, my Lord the King!

6

Sebastien, Sebastien,
What is the faith that flows and fills
Thy heart with strength, thine eyes with light
While ruby-red the life-blood spills?
Look up, look up, O dying Knight —
That faith this blunted arrow kills!

And me . . . No archer thou of His!
Back, back! This death, this suffering
Are but thy sport . . . Lift not my head! . . .
O pale-eyed man, art *thou* the King?

THE QUESTION

Is it enough to feel the opal spring
Burst quivering on branch and bush and wing?
    To kiss the soft-cheeked air?
    To know the world is fair? —
        Is it enough?

Is it enough to see man's passionate
Divinity break shimmering on fate?
    His soul's devout desire
    Flame and go out like fire? —
        Is it enough?

Will beauty and nobility descried,
Will anything save touching hands and side
    Assuage us to confess
    Through life's unhappiness,
        It is enough?

EVENING LINES

Ah, dreamy world and liquid-sounding leaves,
Ah, skies that on your bosom bear the dawn
And evening, and recurrent, trembling stars,
Why are we strangers to your certain calm,
Your joy, perennial and effortless?
We strive to understand; our desperate faith
Leans listening against the universe
To catch some meaning, some deep harmony
To still the throbbing silence that we hear.
In vain, in vain! There is an inner music,
But 'tis no serenade to please our ears.
When the last human heart is underground,
Great sunsets still will aureole the west,
No whit less gorgeous for that they're unseen.
And this divine frail moon will not delay
Because her lovers' lips are yet more pale
Than when her yearning parted them. Ah, no —
Not listeners we, but part, ourselves, of some
Mysterious harmony, perhaps heard elsewhere.

PART II

IN APRIL ONCE, AND OTHER POEMS

III

FROM A SOLDIER'S NOTEBOOK

A VOLUNTEER'S GRAVE

Not long ago it was a bird
    In vacant, lilac skies
Could stir the sleep that hardly closed
    His laughing eyes.

But here, where murdering thunders rock
    The lintels of the dawn,
Although they shake his shallow bed
    Yet he sleeps on.

Another spring with rain and leaf
    And buds serenely red,
And this wise field will have forgot
    Its youthful dead.

And, wise of heart, who loved him best
    Will be forgetting, too,
Even before their own beds gleam
    With heedless dew.

Yet what have all the centuries
    Of purpose, pain, and joy
Bequeathed us lovelier to recall
    Than this dead boy!

NIGHT OFF GALLIPOLI

(EIGHT SPIRIT SONGS)

1

A delirious voice:
    Sweeter than sleep and the dream of death
    To float on the flow of the tempest's breath —
        A leaf in the lift of the air's caresses,
        A bloom in the sway of the sea's brown tresses,
        A bird that the hawk of the storm possesses!
        Death, thou art best,
            Being rest.

2

Voice of a youthful Turk:
    If only up the straits the tempest flew,
    Up the blue waters, past the perilous spray
    To where the clustered cypresses are blue
    Above pale stairs that touch the lisping bay,
    I should not care, I should not greatly care —
    If only up the straits the tempest flew!

    If only up the straits my spirit flew
    As once it flew when sails were all my wings,
    To that deep garden where the moon is blue
    And sea-sounds soften close-lipped whisperings,
    I should not care, I should not greatly care —
    If only up the straits my spirit flew!

Death could not keep me from the arms of you,
But I should die again upon your mouth
While all the swaying garden changed from blue
To red, and softer grew your bosom's south.
I should not care, I should not greatly care,
Dying again upon the mouth of you!

3

An English voice:
      I knew the stars would come,
      Brighter than English stars
And purer than the stars of battle!
      They shine on Thessaly,
      On the pale Argive plain,
And leave a lovelier light on Lesbos.

      O Grecian stars, how oft
      At home, in the grey sea,
I longed to know the lands ye guard!
      Now death, propitious, speeds
      My soul on those dark tides
Whose foam ye lit when Helen fled.

      Blow, wind of Tauris, blow!
      This is the sea that heard
The Lesbian's cry, and further south
      The shining song of him
      Whose heart was washed with tears.
O southward blowing wind, blow on!

4

Voice of a Breton Fisherman:

  Douarnenez! Douarnenez!
O little town on the fishing bay!
O southern sea, too soft, too blue,
  Let me thro'! let me thro'!
Till the green and the cold of the western sea
  And the lonely cliffs of Brittany
And home, my home, Douarnenez,
  Break on mine eyes with the breaking day!

5

Voice of an English poet:

  South! . . . These stars I know! . . . And south is Greece!
O Death, one gentleness I pray —
Let me find rest on that divine, sweet shore,
And have for spirit-home some strip of Hellas!
Some mountain cove in hearing of the sea,
Some fabled fold, perhaps, of Helicon,
Trod once by silver feet, now silvery
With heliotrope and sprinkled sheep,
There bide in quiet death's prepared event. . . .
After the snows, when April nights grow warm
And lilies of the moon blanch field and crag,
When tenderly the wind blows down from Thessaly,
And dews are deep, and down the mountains glide
On feather feet the drifting dreams
Whose land is not the land of sleep —
Ah, then, perhaps, the spirit that incited so
My heart to song in earthlier days,
Balked of the dear delight of utterance,

    Muted beyond all hope of speech,
    May tinge with sharper longing the lament
    Of that sole bird that sings unto his heart,
    Or deeplier dye the coral-mouthèd blooms
    That hide but do not hush the river's brink. . . .

6

A Canadian voice:
    God, God, how well they meant,
    How utterly they failed!
    Why wilt Thou give us strength,
    Courage and fortitude,
    But leave us without reason, impotent?

    They poured us out like water.
    The thirsty ground still drank,
    And still they poured; until
    The hills above the sea
    Were red as sunset, but unconquered still.

    Such blood, so young, so proud!
    No Homer will rise up
    To sing their deeds; for deeds
    There be too great for song,
    And heroes must be few to stir the rage.

    All Canada was Ajax,
    And India, to a man,
    As fierce as Hector was!
    The young isles of the south
    Blazed like Achilles when they killed his friend.

And all for what? For nothing!
We, who in the west
Had crossed perhaps the Rhine,
Have crossed but Lethe here,
And won but failure for our only fame.

There never was a cause
So worthy to be won!
If France and England die,
Freedom and faith are dead —
Give them, O God, not heroes' hearts, but brains!

7

Voice of a French poet:
And so the songs must go unsung,
The dreams be only dreams. . . .
But I have died for France! There is no fate
So worthy them her august blood endues. . . .
When all is said, what is the poet's life?
The vulture's ebb between sky ecstasy
And carrion of earth! Raptured, superb,
He wheels against the sun, then falls
And battens on the refuse beasts refuse!
Somewhere i' the compound, rainbow stuff
And sunset-cloud and green-winged spray,
There creeps the taint, the particle of earth,
That marks it with the black of madness, sin, or quirk.
Only the great are phœnix of the sun,
Unfathered save of flame and dizzy light;

They only keep, unpausingly and pure,
The blue enfeoffments of their gorgeous sire.

Say I had lived; which height had I attained?
The vulture's? Or the phœnix' flaming zone?
Death makes all questions foolish now. . . .
Yet in my soul I know there was a thing in me
Of most immortal lineaments,
Whose speech was beauty and whose thought was
    prayer! . . .
But even so, a year, a hundred years,
A thousand — the loveliest words of men
Are leaves with but a redder tint to time.
The singers pass; the song endures: I die;
But somewhere will gush up the crimson fire
That lit my heart to songs I might not sing.
And there was France to die for! A splendor's there
Beyond the dimming of eternity!
Who would be singer now, not soldier, who
Would live for Fame when he could die for France,
Fame, too, I must believe, will scorn as bastard. . . .
She had no need of songs who asked my life.
Songs! Here was a deed to do
More gracious and more splendid than all songs!
And I have done that deed;
And I am well content.

8

A host of spirits:
    We fought and saw the stars and fell.
        To fight and win were better;
        To fight and fall is well.

Perhaps a god directed so
    We should be overcome;
    Perhaps; we may not know.

We knew the trumpet call of life;
    We knew the call was not
    To victory, but strife.

And if, indeed, no god there be
    That hung the stars we saw,
    Yet we who fought, yea, we

Who died, out on the bloody sod,
    We know beyond all doubt
    In us there was a god.

Strong Spirit, who hast wrought
A fighting world for men,
Take us; like men we fought.

SWALLOWS

(PARIS — MAY, 1918)

Over the roofs the swallows fly
    In the quiet evening air.
Though just above the homes of men,
    They have not any care.

The women on the balconies,
    That watch and seem to see,
The birds could touch them with their wings,
    They stand so quietly.

So quietly! But if the birds
    Had cognizance of pain,
Could hear the prayers that quiver past,
    They would not fly again.

POPPY FIELDS

You say this poppy blooms so red
Because its roots were daily fed
On last year's cold and festering dead?

Such is the blessèd way of earth;
Oblivious, intent on mirth,
To turn rank death to gorgeous birth!

Even this brutal agony,
So hideous, so foul, will be
Romance to others, presently.

And would it not be proud romance
Falling in some obscure advance
To rise, a poppy field of France?

ON LEAVE

I have reached a green, green island
    In a sea without a shore.
Behind the grey waves crumble,
    And I will not look before.

Here there are music and leisure
    And the touch of a tender hand;
Here is my golden river
    And the warm, wide river land.

I am safe to-day, if never;
    They have given me love and rest;
Sailing the sea of sorrow
    I have touched at the isle of the blest.

TO C. P.

Her spirit's loveliness was such
Her body's loveliness I could not see;
I only know her eyes were heavenly blue
That now are grey with tears for me.

IN FRANCE

Let not a foreign earth weigh down my head,
Nor mingle with the dust that was my heart!
Lay me among my own when I am dead,
In my own land, eternally a part
Of all I know and love. I could not sleep
With strangers here, and there is aching need
Of sleep after much weariness, and deep
Were mine at home. It is a place, indeed,
For long, untroubled sleep. All summer there
The pale somnambulists of heaven pass
Immense and silver through the turquoise air,
Trailing their purple garments on the grass.

Though friendless, childless, honorless I come,
They will know I am theirs; they will make room.

THE SOLDIER GENERATION

We are the sons of disaster,
Deserted by gods that are named,
Thrust in a world with no master,
Our altars prepared but unclaimed;
Wreathed with the blood-purple aster,
Victims, foredoomed, but untamed.

Behold, without faith we were fashioned,
Bereft the assuaging of lies;
Thirsty for dreams we have passioned,
Yet more for truth that denies;
Aware that no powers compassioned,
We have turned to our hearts and grown wise.

Leisure we loved and laughter;
Our portion is labor and pain;
For home we are given a rafter
Of wind and a lintel of rain,
And all that our hearts followed after
Is taken and naught doth remain.

Yet never a new generation
But shall live by the battle we fight,
And prosper of our immolation
And reap of our anguish, delight.
Accepting the great abnegation
We are fathers, not children, of light.

Bruised with the scourges of sorrow,
Broke with the terrible rod,
Bidden for respite to borrow
A poppy-red swathe of the sod,
Yet this is our hope — that to-morrow
Will yield of our strivings, God.

AFTER ANY BATTLE

Voice of Earth:
    These are my children's voices! Born
    Not of the sun, who, for a heritage,
    Giveth a light wherewith to see, a fire
    To burn away the dross gat from my loins;
    Nor of the moon whose sons are mad with beauty;
    Nor of the stars, for they, thro' change and drift,
    Behold the steadfast heavens and the pole.
    But these are mine, unfathered and unclaimed,
    Sustained by shining from no sun nor moon
    Nor fixed nor vagrant star.
    Yea, they are mine —
    Dust that is black with my ferocious blood
    And brackish with my tears.
    Their days are short at best, and they return
    With shuddering to my bosom's dark, yet now
    They rob each other of the little years their due,
    And choke the houses of the whimpering dead!
    And why? O why?
    Another's folly wrought this holocaust,
    Calling it falsely by a sacred name,
    Turning the shambles to an altar stone,
    And butchery to sacrifice!

THE SQUIRE

I have sung me a stave, a stave or two,
    I have drunk me a stoop of wine,
I have roystered across a world that was dew
    And a sea that was sunlight and brine.

And now I'll go down where the need is not
    Of a singing heart, but a sword;
I'll fight where the dead men welter and rot
    With the hard-pressed hosts of the Lord.

And should I come back again, 'twill be
    With accolade and spurs,
And many a tale of chivalry,
    And the deeds of warriors.

And should I not, O break for me
    No buds nor funeral boughs —
I go with the noblest company
    That ever death did house.

FOR THEM THAT DIED IN BATTLE

(1914–1918)

How blossomy must be the halls of Death
Against the coming of the newly dead!
How sweet with woven garlands gatherèd
From pastures where the pacing stars take breath!
And with what tender haste, each with his wreath
Of welcome, must the elder dead return
To greet about the doors with dear concern
These much-loved, proud-eyed farers from beneath.
For these that come, come not forspent with years,
Nor bent with long despair, nor weak with tears,
They mount superbly thro' the gold-flecked air,
The light of immolation in their eyes,
The green of youth eternal in their hair,
And Honor's music on them like sunrise.

THE FARM AGAIN

(TO THE 37TH DIVISION)

The dreamy rain comes down,
And cotton's in the grass.
The farmers all complain —
But I watch armies pass. . . .

The ones that did not come
From Ivoiry again
Are marching down the road
And whistling in the rain.

The forty-two I saw
In Olsene, prone and pale,
With packs and helmets on
Pass by me, young and hale.

I hear their laughter plain —
Some blasphemous, quaint jest
That livens up their step
More than an hour's rest.

They talk of Montfaucon,
Of Thielt and Chryshautem;
My cotton rows, it seems,
Are turnip fields to them.

It's hard to stay indoors
With soldiers marching by.

And if you've hiked and fought
It's hard until you die.

. . . . .

Dim Flanders rain comes down,
The cotton's in the grass;
But I watch wistfully
Gay phantom armies pass.

AN EPISTLE FROM CORINTH

Paul of Tarsus, I have enquired of Jesus
And meditated much and read your words
Directed to the wise Corinthians
Of whom am I. There is much beauty in
His life and therefore comfort, and there is beauty
In that unreasoning rush of eloquence
Of yours, so much it almost caught me up
And made me Christian. Such is the power of faith
Ablaze in one we know to be no fool!
I watched you as you preached that day in Athens:
You are no fool, nor saint, but one I judge
Of intellect that somehow has caught fire
And so misleads when it is shiningest.

I had hoped to find in you or in your Christ
Some answer to the questions that unanswered
Slay our wills. . . . There's so much lost!
Parnassus there across the turquoise gulf
Still holds its rose and snow to the blown sun,
But no young Phoebus guides the golden car,
Nor will the years' returning loveliness
For all its perfumed broidure bring again
The Twelve to the bright mountain place they loved.
The gods of Greece are dead, forever dead:
The Romans substitute idolatry;
And there's such peace and idleness in the world
As gives the thinking powers full scope to soar,

And soar they do, but in red-beakèd bands
That darken all the sun and nurture find
On the Promethean bare heart of man.
How strange to see the labor of the world
Straining for plenteous food and drink and warmth,
For ease and freedom and the right to choose,
But winning these win only doubt and anguish!
Is this accessory to our coming here?
Is there no answer waiting to be found?

I judge the struggle for perfection if
Engaged in long enough, say thro' the years
Of gorgeous youth, the ashen middle years,
Will end in calm, a kind of stale content —
No gush and quiver in the leafless tree!
But that's the body's dying, not the fight's
Reward, old age not victory!
Yet who, save those few souls and stern
That passionate unto perfection walk
The alien earth scornful and sure,
Would pledge themselves to life-long virtue
Except exchanged for happiness, here
Or hereafter? Who, I ask and hear no answer.
'Twas for the few that Socrates had thought:
Your Jesus had profounder bitterness
And, wroth against a universal woe,
Conceived a universal anodyne —
Heaven, his father's Kingdom, Paradise.

Hence his success with slave and sick and poor —
The solace for their skimped experience

They find in dreams of restitution and
A promised land, whose king will dower and
Reward their loyalty with bliss eternal.
This promise of his kingdom and the immense
Illusion that he had, shared still by you,
Of coming once again and shortly to
Select mankind for punishment or saving
Are above all the concepts that ensure
His following, which when the fact disproves
Will fall away and be forgotten till
His name will vanish and the careless years
Hide with their passing sandals' dust his dream.

Yet in this Jesus I detect always
Something more true and sound and saving than
The postulates of his philosophy.
Compared with Socrates his intellect
Lacked wonder, self-delight, sufficiency.
The Athenian in his noblest eloquence
Assumed himself a son of God, yet him
I understood, somehow: it seemed at least
Poetically true. But when your Jew
Speaks of his father, all that I never learned
Is near, I cannot think, but I can feel,
And 'spite of me, I have the sense of wisdom
Simpler and fruitfuller and wiser than
All wisdom we had hardly learned before,
That turns irrelevant and pitiful
Much we had frayed and tattered our poor souls
In guessing. Yet when I turn to you for counsel —
And who of his untutored band but you

Is qualified in wide and leisured learning
To parley equal-minded with a Greek? —
I find a blur of words, a wall of thought,
That more completely hide the god I sense
Than the fantastic patter of his humble
Ignorant worshipers . . . Paul, Paul, I'd give
My Greek inheritance, my wealth and youth,
To speak one evening with that Christ you love
And never saw and cannot understand!

But he is dead and you alone are left,
Irascible and vehement and sure,
For me to turn to with the bleak bad question --
Do we then die? Or shall we be raised up? . . .
There is the hope always of other life,
After this choking room a width of air,
A star perhaps after this sallow earth,
After this place of prayer, a place of deeds.
No man but in his heart's locked privacy
Dares hope this muffled transiency we hate
For its most bitter and ignoble failure
Ends not with what our ignorance calls death.
A Christ with promise of eternity
And proof could Christianize a hundred hundred worlds!
There are such glimpses of the never-seen,
Such breathings from the outer infinite,
The possible hath such nobility
As makes us suppliants for further chance —
Not repetition, but more scope, O Powers!

Yet better purposeless mortality
Than this mad answer you proclaim to us.

We shall rise up, you say: so far well said.
This essence that disquieteth itself
With less than truth, that will not tolerate
The fare whereon 'tis fed, but sickens so
For immortalities that it doth shape
Of its own yearning — piteously methinks —
Gods and a dwelling place of distant stars,
This surely hath a strength beyond mere days!
But then you add, with equal certainty,
" There's too a resurrection of the flesh."
This is your creed and final comfort, Jew,
That these our gyves and chains are never slipped,
That this captivity we thought a term
Carks to eternity, do what we will!
The impediments to every high resolve,
The traitors to our nascent deity,
The perfumed, warm, corporeal parts of us
That drug to sleep or death the impetuous will,
These are partakers of such after-life
As our fierce souls may grievously attain!
Tarsus, I'll not accept eternal life
Hampered and foiled by this vile thing of flesh!
There is no fire can burn it pure, no rain
Can wash it clean, no death can scourge it slave!
The spirit that is holier than light
Its touch will stain, its vesture will pollute!

You cannot understand, you are a Jew!
Your pores, unsentient, have never drunk
The perfume of a bush that's red by dawn,
And were you here upon this roof tonight

With Corinth at your feet, you'd never know
It was a night of summer, never feel
The straining on the slender leash of will
At all the murmurs and warm silences.
There's a girl's laugh . . . and footsteps loitering.
You'd never guess why they are slow, nor hear
The half-words breathed, nor smile to find yourself
Wondering if the kiss were mouth or throat. . . .
Perfumes! . . .
The night-wind wakes but to caress,
And kissing sleeps . . . the lover's way. . . .
Gods, gods! This fool would have the harlots' mouth
Immortal as the soul of Socrates!
Forgive me, follower of Jesus. I
Am Greek, all Greek; I know the loveliness
Of flesh and its sweet snare, and I am hurt
At finding nothing where I sought for much.
O Paul, had you been more as other men
Your wisdom had been wiser! Christ, perhaps —
But I was born too late and so miss all.
I see no aim nor end. And yet myself
Hopeless of aught of profit from the fight
Fight on. . . . Perhaps there's something truer than
The truth we can deduce. . . . And after all
Our best is but a turning toward the stars,
An upward gaze. . . .

PART III

ENZIO'S KINGDOM, AND OTHER POEMS

I
LYRICS

Diverging paths we climb,
But if you find a flower
I will applaud its perfume,
I will confess its power.

I seek an amaranth
More lovely than its name,
For me a very heart's rue,
For your hearts not the same.

It blows above the blue
Far-vistaed Paphian sea,
Or so the woman said
Whose green eyes 'sorcelled me.

Joy to you in your meadows,
But I'll search mine alone
And find an amaranth —
Or else a quiet stone.

OCTOBER

These are the days, too few, that I would hold
Of birds that pause before they seek the south,
Of leaves that rustle not, but, dying, fall
In richer beauty than they ever lived,

Of light that is too merciful at last
To be all gold, but aureoles with blue
Or such dim purple as the moon exhales
The wasted brambles and the wounded trees.

Now are untended ways made beautiful
By cobweb flowers, the wistfullest I know,
Rememberers of all forgotten dead —
Wild asters in my country they are called.

At last it is too late for all regret,
Too late for deeds, and dreams hold no reproach,
And might have been is vague as what may be,
And all is well though much has never been.

A CANTICLE

Lovely is daytime when the joyful sun goes singing,
Lovely is night with stars and round or sickled moon,
Lovely are trees, forever lovely, whether in winter
Or musical midsummer or when they bud and tassel
Or crown themselves with stormy splendors in the fall.
But lovelier than day or night or trees in blossom
Is there no secret infinite loveliness behind?

Beautiful is water, running on rocks in mountains,
Or bosoming sunsets where the valley rivers ponder;
Beautiful is ocean with its myriad colors,
Its southern blues and purples, its arctic gray and silver,
Blown into green frost-fretted or wine-dark in the evening.
But still more beautiful than waters calm or cloven,
Than ocean thunder-maned or floored for delicate springtime,
Is there no beauty visible save to our eyes?

Marvellous is the grass, friendly and very clean,
Though intimate with all the dead, the ceaseless dead,
It has great heart and makes the ancient earth forgetful;
It is not troubled by the wind and from the storm
It learns a radiance; all night it wears the dew
And in the morning it is glad with a pure gladness.
More marvellous than dew-strown morning grasses, is there
No brave immortal joyousness that wrought the grass?

Who lifteth in the eastern sky the dark, gold moon?
Who painteth green and purple on the blackbird's throat?

What hand of rapture scattereth sunshine through the rain
And flingeth round the barren boughs of spring returned
Dim fire? Who stenciled with caught breath the moth's wide wing
And lit the ruby in his eyes? Whose ecstasy
Set silver ripples on the racing thunder-cloud
And flared the walls of storm with terrible dead green?
What dreamer fretted dew upon the flat-leafed corn
And twined in innocence of useless perfect art
The morning-glory with its bubble blue, soon gone?
Was there no hand that braided autumn branches in
Their solemn brede and stained them with a sombre rust?
Was there no love conceived the one-starred, rivered evening,
And dipped in crocus fire the gray horns of the moon?

They say there never was a god men loved but died —
Dead is Astarte, Astoreth is dead, and Baal;
Zeus and Jehovah share a single grave and deep;
Olympus hears no laughter, Sinai no voice;
Spring comes, but Freia comes not nor Persephone:
On temple plinth and porch the random grasses run;
Of all their priests alone the white-stoled stars are faithful.
Dead are the gods, forever dead! And yet — and yet —
Who lifteth in the eastern sky the dark, gold moon? . . .
There is a loveliness outlasts the temporal gods,
A beauty that, when all we know as beautiful
Is gone, will fashion in delight the forms it loves,
In that wide room where all our stars are but a drift
Of glimmering petals down an air from far away.

TO ONE DYING

When you are gone the stars will be content,
Gazing as always in the deep of ocean;
There will not be a fluttering bird that cries
With anguish more importunate beneath the moon;
The rolling seasons with unhindered flow
Of bloom and scarlet tatterings and feathered ice
Will fold the world in loveliness as now.
But I shall have but these, and these with glory shorn
And half invisible because you went. . . .
Then I shall pass. And none because of me
Will be less glad of spring or watch with eyes that blur
The evening's one bright star.
Only, I think, in some remote demesne
That you have learned to love regretfully
There will be added brightness and a cry
Of patient waiting done.

COURAGE

Into a brown wood flew a brown bird
    In the winter time:
The sky was dark with snow unfallen,
    The leaves were bent with rime.

Once north he flew, once south he flew,
    He perched in a naked tree.
He looked into the dismal dusk
    And whistled merrily.

HIS PEACE

I love to think of them at dawn
Beneath the frail pink sky
Casting their nets in Galilee
And fish-hawks circling by.

Casting their nets in Galilee
Just off the hills of brown,
Such happy, simple fisherfolk
Before the Lord walked down.

Contented, peaceful fishermen,
Before they ever knew
The peace of God that filled their hearts
Brim-full, and broke them too.

Young John who trimmed the flapping sail,
Homeless, in Patmos died.
Peter who hauled the teeming net,
Head-down, was crucified.

The peace of God, it is no peace,
But strife closed in the sod.
Yet, brothers, pray for but one thing,
The marvellous peace of God.

HYMN OF THE MAGDALENE

I could not see the morning stars He made,
Nor hear the morning birds who pray aloud;
The flowers were not my brothers nor the winds
Who blow the silver-linèd trees to cloud.

No light upon the hills, no purple bloom
Behind the lifting moon in summer time;
No sweetness in the everyday of life,
No peace, no tears, no rest in Fancy's clime.

But now my sin is done and I can lift
Mine eyes unto the mansions that He made,
And I am wrapped about with holiness
And drenched in glories that can never fade.

Yea, I have put mine olden sin away
And broke and strewn my heart beneath His feet;
His wisdom robbeth me of any fear,
His tenderness upon my mouth is sweet.

O holy light upon the sacred hills,
O birds that flash above the flowered sod,
O clean, immortal beauty of the earth,
I have returned to you and to my God!

BETH MARIE

Impatiently she drew her breath,
    So new was life, so wild:
But patiently she waited death
    And when he touched her, smiled.

She who had never wished to die,
    Who had such fear of pain,
Was tranquil as an evening sky
    That flowers from spent rain.

For us her loss was different
    From all we could suppose:
The calm of Spartan stars she lent
    Who only seemed a rose.

AUTUMN SONG

Time was when billowy autumn skies
    And red rain-dabbled leaves
Would fling the tears across my eyes.
    'Tis happiness that grieves.

Now lengths of scarlet-littered rain
    May lash the howling eaves;
My eyes are casual as pain.
    'Tis happiness that grieves.

FOR A WORD

How shall you ever know the adoration
I spread like samite cloths beneath your feet?
How shall you guess the brooding desolation
Learned from your eyes so passionless and sweet?

There must be some word like the star that pauses
In summer's rose transparency of dusk,
Or like the bird-note heard through slumber's gauzes
The unsilvering hour before dew warms to musk.

There must be some one word that is more tender
Than any word my lips have ever learned,
Without which I can never, never render
In speech the love your cool sweet love has earned.

You know as none my heart's forlorn distresses,
Its passionate tides, its daily tint and glow, —
Why must there be within obscure recesses
This tenderness of love you cannot know?

SAFE SECRETS

I will carry terrible things to the grave with me:
    So much must never be told.
My eyes will be ready for sleep and my heart for dust
    With all the secrets they hold.
The piteous things alive in my memory
    Will be safe in that soundless dwelling:
In the clean loam, in the dark where the dumb roots rust
    I can sleep without fear of telling.

YOUTH

When I look on the youth of the world I weep:
Their eyes are so shadowless and candid,
They run so eagerly to meet the future,
They are so beautiful even in their passions —
So restless to live, so fickle, so yearning;
They have such faith in happiness,
Such songs in their hearts, such dreams in their eyes.
The light of them shines like light on the meadows,
Their laughter is sturdy and full of innocence;
Their vehemence, their proud assurance,
And most, their sweetness and their happiness
I watch till my eyes are blurred with pity.
For they will learn and wither with their learning;
Their flower look will die a flower's death.
And one will learn of love and one of want
And one of death and one of weakened will,
But all will learn and all will weep alone.
There will be no shining left for death to darken,
And their lovely throats and eyes will not be lovely
Before the dust corrodes them, long before.
Cold pain will kiss them and they will not smile
As once they smiled when peach-blow kisses fell;
And fear will blanch the red run of their blood,
And doubt uncurve the bow of their sweet mouths,
And tears that were a gust of gold-shot rain
Will turn a brackish drink for their poor hearts,
And they will know what we have known too long.
Spare them, O heartless gods who spared not us!

SIGHT AND SOUND

I saw a handful of white stars
Blooming in a width of grass;
I saw a cherry tree, snow-white,
In woods as naked-cold as glass.

I saw a blue leaf zigzag down —
The bluebird with his russet throat!
From out the sallow cane-brake stole
Another bluebird's aching note.

The blue, the white, I wrote them down
To soothe my heart when spring was over.
No need, or help, alas, to write
That bluebird's " Lover, lover, lover! "

SHE GRIEVES IN THE DUSK

Ah, he was white and slender
And the lamplight turned him gold
And his groping hands were tender
And his kisses never bold.
How shall I sleep through the long, long nights
In my wide cold-sheeted bed,
Hearing the wild geese crying in their flights,
And me afraid,
And him not by to turn and hold me to his heart
In the way he knew,
And me no longer folded to his heart,
Thinking him true!

AFTERGLOW

Limpid lavender like water-hyacinths
The light floods on after the sun is down
And tips ethereally the primrose moon.
There is a delicate music in the films of the air,
And I remember how I saw, long, long ago,
A primrose slip of a girl, with lowered lids
And fugitive smile such as Luini loved,
Flush ethereally with the flooding of first love.

THE UNLOVED TO HIS BELOVED

        Could I pluck down Aldebaran
           And haze the Pleiads in your hair
I could not add more burning to your beauty
Or lend a starrier coldness to your air.

        If I were cleaving terrible waters
           With death ahead on the visible sands
I could not turn and stretch my hands more wildly,
More vainly turn and stretch to you my hands.

A MAD MAID'S SONG

Here's tansy for you, and a sprig of rue.
Such simples are not worn upon the brow,
    But next a heart they'll keep it true —
        Or did till now.
    A sprig of rue should keep it true
    And tansy's good as any vow.
    But round your heart, not round your brow
    Wear them, and wear enough for two.

EXCHANGE

It does not seem a piteous thing to pass
From out the passionate sunlight and to never see
    Light-loving winds press down the tremulous grass
        Inconstantly.

The closing of the eyes, the clean forgetting,
The silence broken by no whispering love-calls,
    These willingly I'd take — not once regretting
        Unheard footfalls.

What power lies in long, untender kisses
To steal the tears from pain, the innocence from mirth!
    What loved exchange — these desolate, hurt blisses
        For folded earth!

A DEBUSSY SERENADE

    Love, they say, is kind:
        Nay, wrinkles here
  And here love gave to me
        And quenched my eyes.
    Love is not kind.

  A god, they say, is love.
      Do gods, then, dull
The aureate dawn and bleach
      The purple haze?
    No god is love.

  A boy, they say, is love.
      His hunter's eyes,
Alert and cold, I saw,
      Insatiable,
    And they were old.

  Give back, O love, give back
      What you have stole,
And I will make return
      Of all your gifts —
    And go, enriched.

WINDS OF WINTER

Shake out, dark-tressed and multitudinous storm-winds,
Your theft of scarlet leaves for Hecate's hair,
Your coral bits from autumn's dead clenched hand,
Your brittle blooms that once had breath and color,
Asters and docks and hateful immortelles —
Scatter them down, but bear away the summer
And hopes that were and loves that could not be.
Strip off the garlands, hang the trees with fire
Of frost and clanking armor of blue ice.
There is much death abroad and for a tomb
Starkness were needed and unmelted tears.
Welcome, dark-tressed and multitudinous storm-winds.

HYMN TO THE SUN

Strike down into my breast, O sun, and cleanse my soul —
    Shadows are here and ailments of the dark!
    Burn out the horror, sear away the dread,
    Beat like live hope in spark on molten spark.

Lone in your uncouth solitude of chasmed air
    You scale the sky, reckless of end or change,
    Chanting like some wild Himalayan shepherd
    Wind-rocked, enraptured, on his bleak vast range.

Eternity will pass and down the blue cliffs hear
    You singing, vigorous still in fierce delight.
    Strike through my breast and pour your courage in —
    Enough to last this little way to night.

COMPENSATION

Delicious hurt is in the throb
Of every ruby in youth's blood:
Moonlight or love can call a sob,
Or red trees in a drizzling wood.

We own a strength we never guess
When warm and weak with April's wine,
A fortitude against the stress
Of tragic things young hearts divine.

The visions that we could not bear
Turned facts are borne almost with grace:
The future with its heartbreak air
Arrives unflushed and commonplace.

Far-travelled in the land of pain,
Fate's clear worst warrant learned by rote,
I watch the red trees in the rain
With eyes undimmed and unhurt throat.

THAT KINGDOM

Fingerless cactus hands heal in the sun
And tortured olive trees grope up the hills;
A lizard feigns to sleep but flinching kills
The busy spider in her web half done.

The gaunt Sicilian pastures burn blue-white,
The sunlight rains its blue perpetual rain;
The south is still the south, but not again
Shall I find there my kingdom, Heart's Delight.

Oh, not on hills of blue eternal lustre
Build we the kingdom of our heart's delight,
But on love's shale, that quakes above a night
Where ocean yawns and screaming storm-birds cluster.

AUTUMN WISDOM

The nights of autumn stars are never still,
For without gust the heavy acorns fall
And rattle on the roof — the oak's proud gift
And happy show of his accomplishment.

For this he shouldered storms and stripping hail,
For this unwrinkled in the weak spring sun
His velvet buds and shook his tassels out
And ruffled noisily in boisterous May.

For this — a fall of acorns in the starlight.
But where they fall, what burgeoning or death
Awaits them on the sparkling, plangent ground
Are not to his bronze peace inquietudes.

On glittering shale, perhaps, or sterile sand
Their hope of swelling spring will waste away;
Perhaps the droves of night-marauding hogs,
Scuffling and loud, will eat the last smooth one;

Perhaps the little children, up at dawn,
Scouring the deep-rimed leaves for treasure-trove,
Will set them with their spools and broken glass
For patterns in their fairy palaces;

Perhaps not one will burst and branch and grow
A windy place for elf-eyed boys to climb,

A shade for clasping lovers in the night,
A spangled roof for old folk in the rain.

He will not care: his joy is to have done
The appointed deed, not guess the deed's result.
Along his branches creeps the bright-eyed frost.
He spills his fruit and laughs against the stars.

ONE PATH

Outside the Earthly Paradise,
    Beneath its cool high walls,
I walk the little grass-blurred path
    Where sunlight seldom falls.

I try no more the guarded gates
    That will not let me in;
I cease to wonder what the cause,
    What accident, what sin.

I walk the lonely path that's mine,
    My heart and I employ
Our solitude in songs about
    The near-by Kingdom's joy.

And once, while singing thus, we heard
    Applause and friendly cries,
And saw, high up, our happy kin,
    Love in their lovely eyes.

The path of lonely wayfaring
    Ends where I cannot tell:
Outside the Earthly Paradise
    I know — but that is well.

TO A STRANGER

When I see your beauty the beasts in me lie down
And I know the good man that I might have been.
To watch you is more cleansing than clear sunsets
And more regretful than the deeds that I have done.
If memory could only keep me perfect
And not fade out to leave me with myself!
With all my altars ashes and my gods asleep
You with your marvellous sad infinite beauty
Make me kneel down and know what life could be —
Unhurtfulness and worship and sure trust.
But I have missed you in the passing of the ships
And as a stranger only watch you pass.
Yet seeing you tonight in your great beauty
I shall dream calmly of a clear green sky
Filled with wild white swans flying, flying over,
Against the hardly-visible, wide-swarming stars.

WONDER AND A THOUSAND SPRINGS

    Along the just-returning green
    That fledges field and berm and brake
    The purple-veined white violets lean,
        Scarcely awake;

    And pear and plum and apple trees,
    Evoked to bloom before they leaf,
    Lift cloudy branches filled with bees
        Strange as new grief.

    A thousand springs will poise and pass
    And leave no track beneath the sun:
    Some gray-eyed lad, cool-cheeked as grass,
        Will watch each one,

    And wonder, as I wonder here,
    And find no clue I have not found,
    And smile before he joins me, near
        But underground.

CALYPSO TO ULYSSES

If there were any room within my heart
For godly pride to linger, I should not kneel
And clasp your feet. But there's no tenant here
Save love, and he has made me your idolater.

I am alone, belovèd, but for you.
Cast out the sea-look from your eyes and look
On me, my utter self — no luring left,
No unused wile to whet your appetite.

You know me all, and all of me is yours.
I should have kept some harlot reticence
To bate the surfeiting beast in you. Alas!
Shrink not. Men's modesty is but in speech.

These are still gray eyes and pomegranate lips
As once you called them, whispering through my hair
In the dawn-stillness when the dawn-bird sang,
And blissfully your drowsy kisses clung.

What is the loss that loses me your favor,
Your misty voice, your eyes spilled full of color,
Your hands whose very stillness in a curve
Betrayed their greediness to reach for mine?

Ah, do you dream, lover no longer young,
That those frail ecstasies can be lived over

If only on some new young breast you slumber
And fresher lips yearn to you in the dark?

There is no second spring: your first is past
And it was passed with me and you are mine!
Or can a woman never claim as hers
The heart of any man before it breaks?

Oh, is the love of man a sunset waning,
A music slipping by, a one day's flower,
Its very fleetingness the magic flaw
That lures the fixed idolatrous love of woman?

Say not it is the sea that summons you,
Or such affairs as chafing heroes plan:
Hearted as that fierce pleading wanderer
That once was you, nothing could draw you from me!

Belovèd, leave me not! There is such terror
In the loneliness of souls that once were large!
Though yours be never lonely, without you
Mine were a gray rock in a wintry sun.

No use, no use! The touch of you tells me that.
This body that I gave you when the gift
Was begged as sole alternative to death
Has served and staled. . . . The sea calls and you go.

Then go. . . . No, I should hate a sea-cold kiss;
Remembered ones will do. . . . And I'll endure
Loneliness with more profit and more pride
Than you an aging man's concupiscence.

SPRING NIGHT IN THE MOUNTAINS

The lakes of the sky are clearer than day
    And all but the great stars are drowned,
The glorying winds and the phosphorous clouds
    Fling the dark in swift coils on the ground,
And the burning bleared moon in a halo of bronze
    Is dashed through the zenith like sound.

It should be cold when the trees are so bare
    Or the breezes spring-gentled for flight,
Not torturing thus the dogwood that writhes
    Like a desperate immaculate light.
I am afraid of the night and the spring
    And the terrible winds of the night!

Afraid of the rapture that grapples and tears
    Till the cords of my heart are torn,
While the moonlight is crashing down canyons of cloud
    Like blasts from a great silver horn,
And all the impenitent lovers, long dead,
    Are blown past, lip to lip, unforsworn.

SIREN SONG

These are the seaward cliffs: let us sing and forget.
The daylight dazzles upon us, cloudless and clean,
And there, far down, where the crimson rocks are wet,
Shallows mottle the sapphire sea with green.
      Come, let us forget,
And, healed of ancient tears and whole of ancient teen,
    Sing with cold hearts of joy and no regret.

Fair from safe hill-tops seem the passing sails,
Fairer perhaps because they always pass,
And that far mountain-land, that quakes and pales
In the noon stillness, fair too and far, alas!
      No rough sweet hails
Will glitter up our glens, nor will a bruised bright grass
    Betray some parting's anguish in our vales.

We are accursed. Why should our thoughts yet cling
To them that loved us when they knew us not,
But learning us despised? Come, let us sing
Forgetfully, loving this lovely spot
      Where the swallows swing
Half down the cliff white-breasted, shrill, and the haze is hot
    Plumbago blue like a witch's eyes in spring.

Not the wind's fingers scribbling on the floor
Of ocean write a rune more incomplete
And mad than that fate marked above the door

Of our strange hearts, set open to all feet.
        Oh, seek no more
Its meaning. Sing, let our songs be ignorantly sweet
          Like upland waters pluming as they pour.

Alas! no music sounds here save our tears
And all things we have won except forgetfulness!
          Our longing veers
      Back to the native land of our distress —
            No sights may bless
      Eyes the red needle of endurance sears.
Then let us sing again with heartbreak wise and mad
The terrible songs we sang once ere we came,
And win the round windy ocean that was glad
To be one sorrowing echo of our shame.
        Never, never, never may we unlearn
          The secret with which we burn,
              Never appease
        Our mortal hurt with these
            Felicities.
                Again
          Lift we our voices,
      Our music old with bitterness and bane,
For we weave our songs and our songs are woven
            Of pain,
And the heart that sings is the heart that is cloven.

A LETTER

Aid my heart in its fidelity!
Though my unfaith were no regret to you
It would betray, O careless heart I love,
Not only you, but love itself, and me.
That I am absent brings no pain to you,
But every hour away is death to me —
Send me some word, though heartless as your love,
And aid my heart in its fidelity.

AFTER HEARING MUSIC

Give me a breath of air!
There is too much of sweetness here,
Too much of pain, pain blent with loveliness.
I am allured from all that we call living
And sickened of the harsh necessities.
The earth again! the earth where sweat is poured
To rise in bronze ripe undulant fields of grain,
Where here and now is sinewed hardihood
And intertwining effort vain and vast.
What now is Avalon, or purple ships that plow
The dim blue evening full of mists and tears?
Give me a breath of air, a sound of voices,
For I am drugged with dreams
And smothered with the smoke of old disasters.
Of what avail dead lovers laid in Avalon
Or purple ships outbound?

IN THE COLD BRIGHT WIND

Merlin, Merlin's gone away
    With a limmer witch for spouse,
He's gone to spend a sorry year
    In the Queen o' Fairies' house.

For gear he's took the sapphire bird
    Wi' the bubble in his throat;
His hat was prinked wi' the wee wet flowers
    That gaud daft April's coat.

Sunny-cold the bold wind blew
    As he strode off down the hill;
His red cloak bellied out and swirled,
    His eyes burned gray and chill.

For promise of a warm high bed
    And spiced renewing drink
He's footed it to Fairyland
    Where love's the only swink.

He's gone away, and not alone —
    Brightly, oh, he sinned!
His red cloak glimmers on the thorn
    And his laughter on the wind.

THE GREEN BIRD SEETH ISEULT

    A green bird on a golden bush,
        And the leaves chimed out and spake:
    " What have you seen, what heard, green bird,
        Since you heard the blue day break? "

    " A sea, a sea, a saffron sea,
        And a creamy warm full sail
    Floating beneath me as I flew,
        And my shadow stamped the sail
    Like a clover leaf, a green clover leaf,
        Blown from an Irish dale."

    " Did lovers pale stand by the sail
        That furrowed the Irish sea?
    Did you catch the glimmer of golden mail
        And the glimmer of hair blown free? "

    " Golden each scale of his burnished mail
        And her hair was bronze and gold:
    From an emerald cup I saw them sup
        That their four hands scarce could hold."

    " Delight and woe, delight and woe,
        Bird of the Irish sea —
    These they drank up from the emerald cup
        On the sun-swooned saffron sea."

" Only delight, only delight,
While the beautiful burning blue daylight
  Was dappled by me
With the green leaf-shadow shapen in three.
Delight I saw, delight I heard! "
Sang the sunlight-aureoled emerald bird
  To the golden tree
   Deliriously.

AVERNEL

From Avernel the hills flow down
    And leave it near the sky,
And it has birds and bells and trees
    And fauns that never die.

When coral-pink azaleas fill
    Its roomy woods with sweet,
And lilac spills of violets wait
    For violet-veined swift feet;

When moths are budded by the oaks'
    Uncrinkling rose and red
And high, high up, green butterflies
    Reveal the poplars' head;

When shaggy clouds in single bliss
    Blaze up the sea-blue air,
Spilling their shadow-amethyst
    Along the hills' wide stair;

Then there is singing in the sun
    And whispering in the shade
And dancing till the stars slope down
    Their murmurous arcade.

In love's half sleep the curly faun's
    Uncertain if he sees
Orion or first fireflies
    Between the clear dark trees.

CANOPUS

When February brings the hopeless days
And there's no cranny of the silent world
Where grass is green or boughs are fresh
Or birds recall their litanies of love,
And earth seems but a place where graves are dug
And dug too tardily —
Then turn for peace to those forgotten stars
That change not with the changes of the year,
But still pursue their purposed ministries
In the cold night,
Though loveliness lies dead upon the ground.
Then their serene proud ranks receive
From thick-starred equatorial climes
A lone and flaming guest,
The lord and love of all the southern sky.
Above, aye, just above the black horizon
When the first dark is clear,
You see him rise, superb and alien,
The fiery-haired Canopus, surging from the south.
But one vast scornful stare he flings
Across the full curve of the northern night
Wherein Arcturus and Aldebaran
Marshal the bright-helmed sons of heaven;
Then, meeting the blue gaze of Sirius,
Turns, and retreating down the crystal dark
Hides from our eyes his haughty slow return.
The serpentining Amazon

And many a lost lagoon, flamingo-stirred,
Mirror his golden shaggy hair;
The wide-palmed plantain-leaves
Receive in sleep his tread,
And glimmer, dreaming that the moon glows past;
In their rough pastures
Bronze Peruvian shepherds mark his course
And call his name, and vainly call.
For he strides on in his dim godly wrath
Past Ecuador
And the long samite carpet of the Argentine.
Past the incredible drear rooms of stone
The Incas built, by night, to helpless gods,
On precipices of the fearful Andes;
Nor stays his step till he descries, far down,
The ghostly mountainous antipodes,
Mute with blue cold.
There, trembling in his wreath of flames, he halts
And gazes on the glistering nether pole
Where his reflection shakes —
Contemplative
And sunk in his own thought.
But then our land is gay with polished leaves
And birds are nesting in the calm sweet sun.

FRENCH BLUE

There's a blue flower grows in France
    A tattered roadside thing,
Like flowers cut, by little girls,
    Of paper while they sing,

Which when I see so far from home
    I feel tears almost rise,
For it is blue with just the blue
    Of one dear lady's eyes.

FOR A POET'S BIRTHDAY

The plowman breaks the smelling earth
    And birds are in his wake;
He scatters seed for harvesting,
    They, song for singing's sake.

His heedful heart is happy as
    Their hearts that take no heed —
But happiest the furrow's heart
    Where song is sown with seed.

A PORTRAIT

When I see you I think of Mary, the mother of God,
Before she was a mother. But you are older,
Though young, so young that when I think of Calvary
I do not see you fainting at the cross
But bending over her who faints, your arms
About her, your tears upon her face, your voice
Comforting, were there comfort in the world.
Yet there's no beauty of the sweet-aired earth
Not reminiscent to my heart of you:
Water, the very pure winds of heaven, and the dew,
Birds at their matins, all limpid-colored flowers,
Not those that blaze in peacock opulence,
But such compassionate and candid blooms
As hurt the throat: branches of half-blushed peach,
Anemones that have a just-born air,
Miraculous, blue, breathless morning-glories,
Crocuses far too cool to be like flames,
And cosmos only of the autumn host.
These certainly I know to be your kin.
Yet this, your outward self, could dull and tarnish
And still your loveliness would be no less
And still men could not fail to see in you
That which they always hope to find in women —
The unnameable gay goodness that they love,
Attained in tears, most evident in smiles,
And more worth dying for than creed or crown. . . .
No wonder, seeing you, I think of Mary,
The mother of God, before she was a mother.

RAIN PATTER

The lambs are sleeping in the rain
Cuddled two and two together,
One alone might sleep in pain
On the hillside in such weather.
In the spring rain slow and steady,
Just before the leaves are ready,
Walking is contentment's gain,
That is, walking with another,
Best a lover, then heart's brother —
All alone might waken pain.
Come then, dear, be wise again,
Ramble with me in the soft spring rain —
Walking is contentment's gain!
We'll see weeping willow's mane
Beaded with the moonstone rain,
Then the oat-field's emerald stain,
Then a brambled dripping lane
Where johnny-jump-ups, pert and plain,
Are common as the inch-high grain.
If walking's more than going's art
Unaided by curt car or cart,
Your eyes a thief, a sleuth your heart,
We'll find, I have no doubt at all,
Right in the cold wood's hollow cove
Branches of blurry pink I love —
(The red-bud always has his anguish out
Before the leaves are there to laugh and flout).

We'll surely see a redbird fall
And hear, if you'll not breathe at all,
The tentative self-conscious call
Of the young mockingbird who slyly
Practises when he sings not shyly
At windows and from garden borders
When what he sings is what he orders.
(But men have lived and died quite near
And never heard his muted fear,
So exquisite and faint and clear.)
What if I should show to you
A plum tree and a cherry too,
Both white as lilies Mary grew,
And hazed about with rain?
Oh, if we go as I like best,
Haphazardly and with a zest,
You'll have no need to seek for pleasure
In lands that other daytimes measure,
But every bush will be your treasure!
Come out, come out, be wise again
Before the spring begins to wane —
There's nothing gladder, I maintain,
Than walking together in the rain!

MEDITATING A JOURNEY

    The swallows curling in the sky,
    Less wishful to be gone than I,
    Well know the land whereto they fly
        In fickle flight.
    To bathe in sun-soothed southern air,
    Where one cloud-shadow is as rare
    As true love, is their only care
        And sole delight.
    But I, what south could I attain
    That would not seem a journey vain
    When all my sun doth here remain,
        How coldly bright!

ITALIAN SUMMER

Tiberius is in his grave,
But where that is who's saying?
It's long and long since hereabouts
Poppaea went a-maying.

Oh, all the hearts that on this breeze
Brush by like motes of gold!
The many a tear, the many a kiss
No secret to this mold!

Oh, let's not let the lovely dead
Distract us from our passion —
They are so dead, so soon we'll be!
Love passes like a fashion.

Palazzo di Tiberio

DELIGHT

Delight it is has kept me
From thinking much, I fear,
And I'd have loved more wisely
Had not delight been near;
And tears a few he's cost me,
But saved me many a tear.

O friends that I have clung to
To save me from time's spite,
O loves of mine whom kissing
I've wished all time were night —
I'd keep you all, but lose you
Before I'd lose delight!

ADVICE IN SPRINGTIME

When evening skies are smoked with rose,
And dubious spring behind the hill
To come or not a thistle blows,
And buds amaze wet puckered snows —
Then watch your will, your lazy will,
For then he loves to sleep his fill.

He yawns if yearning's in the breeze,
Nods at violets paused before,
And should you watch with soft unease
The sad blood-pink of Judas trees,
He's sleeping sure, content to snore
At warm temptation's very door.

To nunneries, you maidens all!
You old despairs of saving grace,
Young men so lusty-limbed and tall,
To desert caves and diets small!
For earth's a shameful, sighful place
Beneath the unwimpled spring's embrace.

INSOMNIA

O little boats of Capri
That fish a mile from town
And nick the dark with torches
Till heaven is upside-down,

I may forget these brown warm eyes,
These brown throats as they turn,
These girls with burdens on their heads
Like Greek girls on an urn;

Their dark-lashed, rascal sweetness,
Their smiles I may forget, —
But not your constellations
Splashed gold on miles of jet.

Above you Mars and Spica
Curve down into the sea,
Springing from you the Scorpion's vine
Festoons the heavenly tree.

May all your nets be silver-chocked,
May all your sails win through!
In each of you were sleepless eyes
When mine were sleepless, too.

SUBLIMATION

Lock your sin in a willow cage,
    Cover the key with clay:
Hanging beneath your rafters' shade
    He'll sing for you some day.

Outside your good deeds cluck and strut,
    But small's the joy they bring.
It's only a wistful prisoner bird
    With a wicked heart can sing.

Break not the lock, bend not the withes!
    Escaping through some chink,
His song will cease — in your live heart
    His beak will take its drink.

FOUR CAPRI IMPROMPTUS

1

Sweet as the furze flower fainting in the noon heat,
The yellow furze flower tufted in a cliff above the ocean,
Floating its too sweet perfume over the peacock waters
And weakening the diving swallows half down the air —
So sweet, so weakening the breath of you comes to me, belovèd,
When I lean over you, or even, even when I dream of you, my flower.

2

Mournful and miraculous beauty bathes the sea
When the rose-misted sun melts out,
And for one perfect moment —
While two swallows can eddy and plunge their white breasts
From the cliff-crest to the beach —
The waters are misty rose for infinite miles
Save for the silver chariot-tracks of the winds;
Curving and leading nowhere and always silver,
But edged, how strangely, with keen victorious green.

3

Just over the gray cliffs
In the blue brumal air
Glistens a faint unwilling Hesper,
His curls bound with a fillet of white fire.
Along the sky his steps seem slow

Like a young sulky god's,
So I should see him as he stands a moment
Dreamily on the cliff top, between the two twisted stone-pines.
There he may pause and watch the blue lilies of the twilight
Like sleep-flowers on the fields of the still sea,
Blue-gray like sleep-flowers on the mountain flanks
And the coves of the unwindy coming night.
There I have stood on other evenings
Watching a long time the lonely twilight.
But the young Hesper has no heart to look.
Barely I saw his silver instep touch the top
And he was gone —
Running, running, not pausing for a glance,
Down the dark other side of the sheep-strewn cliff.
He is no shepherd:
He had no tawny wisp of net over his arm,
No net to cast in the foam-flowered breakers from the beach
Like a fisher-boy.
I think he has some love far down on the tilted side in the darkness
To whom he hurries —
A nymph perhaps, maybe another star
With floating hair and a girl's silver body.
Surely with such a single amorous haste
Before the night is over,
Even before the Pleiads tremble up,
He will be with her,
Lying, I dare say, greedily,
The sweat-beads pearling still the curve of his shoulders
And his breast still heaving.

4

I shall bring you blue morning-glories ribbed with purple,
Or hazy-blue plumbago flowers.
But they will not please you: they have no perfume.
Shall I search higher and twitch a spray of golden gorse?
The bees cannot leave it
And it is sweeter and more golden than their honey.
Or I know a cleft above the sapphire ocean
Where grows one shoot of the wild oleander.
Its flowers are crimson pink:
Some say it is Adonis' blood that they are dipped in,
Others, more rightly, Aphrodite's own.
And their perfume when full open in the noon heats
Has often made a passing dryad drowsy.
Pan never nears their shadow except on tiptoe —
He has made lucky finds in their sleepy shade.
But you — none of these will content you,
Neither the blue morning-glories
Nor ash-blue clusters of plumbago
Nor gorse that is golden yellow
Nor blood-rose oleanders.
How shall I hope that my heart may please you
Which is less lovely than these,
But not less quickly withered?

AN ARCADIAN IDYLL

Far, far from here,
Above Andritsaena,
In the naked hills that paling darkness covers,
A sandalled goatherd climbs the path
Behind his flock.
Vacant the sleeping pastures,
For the bees, too, still are sleeping,
Vacant and thick with dew and flower-strown,
Tempting to bearded goats.
Slowly he follows them,
Thongs criss-cross to his knees,
With short Arcadian skirt,
A stripling, brown and roughened by the sun.
Limpid breezes,
Running slim fingers through his burnt black hair,
Have touselled it to elf-locks;
Slender and straight,
His thighs are hardened to the upward pull.
Companionless he goes, half insolent,
His crook behind his shoulders,
A smile behind his lips,
A tuft of golden crocus buds
In one cold hand.
His arrogant unamorous eyes, brook-brown,
Scorn to laugh, though flickering with laughter.
The pasture ground is reached,
A rocky hillside, rank with asphodel,

Beneath the temple ruin shepherds know —
Bassae, the healing god's gray windy house.
The flock apprize the field with yellow eyes,
Shallow and cold,
Then scatter, some
On hind legs reaching for the wet cool buds
Of stunted trees,
Some browsing where the scentless heliotrope
Patterns the ground with white and lilac bloom.
Below,
The brook sends up a breezy sound
From clustered laurel trees
That gad its mirrory lengths along
To watch the crimson fillets of their buds,
That smell and open to the passionate sun.
He stops, lays down his crook,
Then, catching up the world in one sure glance,
Draws from his leathern belt
The uncouth shepherd's flute,
Perches him on a ledge of seeded grasses
And, knees drawn up,
Fills it with steady breath.
His cheeks swell out;
His neck strains into chords,
Crimsons beneath the tan;
His mischievous eyes tilt upward in delight,
And raucous happy sounds insult the dawn.

Shadows whisk in the temple portico,
Advance on shaggy feet,
Drop down, again advance,

Scurry from bush to bush,
And crowd at last
The crest of hills that half encircle him
Noisy below.
But he pipes on and only hears his piping,
And never sees for all his laughing glances
Flat in the dew, with chin on hand and ears pricked up,
Biting a wisp of feathered grass,
The little wood-gods
Listening.

A BRITTANY IDYLL

Far, far from here,
By Tristan's isle,
The bay awaits the breeze,
Paler than harebells breathed on by the dew,
Paler than turquoise, for the dawn is young
And single stars yet shine above Douarnenez. . . .
An easterly wind at sunset blew the fishing fleet
From its safe harborage beneath the town
Into the sunset.
With single sails they flew,
Yellow and brown and carmine-stained,
Across the blinding mirrors of the bay,
Beneath the tawny sunset flared with blue,
Beyond the western portals of the world.
But where the cold Atlantic waters, hoar and black,
Catch on their sleek enormous rhythms slurs of stars,
They lowered sail, and rocked upon the swell.
Then nets were cast and glimmering sank,
And night long, with few words
But mighty laborings,
The fisher-folk hauled in the flickering catch.
Beneath the stars they toiled, on ocean's floor.

But now the night is passing,
Leaving a silver wake
And aster petals halfway up the sky.
It is a lover's sunrise:

Lavender and gray and shining pink,
A tilted sea-shell's inner opulence.
Beyond the jetty that the town throws out
For harborage and home to little boats,
The concave waves are dappled with rose leaves
And floats of foam.
At the jetty's end, far out from shore,
Nearest the point where turning in
From open water to calm anchorage
The fishing-fleet sails past,
A girl is standing.
And only she and the sunrise and wavering gulls
See the curves of rustling tide run in
And hear the calm world's breathing.
She is not lonely
For all her loneliness,
There in the summer sunrise,
With her simple peasant's dress of black,
Her meagre shawl of black crochet,
And her peasant's cap, looped and starched and white,
Prim on her pale gold hair.
Her arms are idly spread across the coping,
Her eyes turn always seaward, for she knows
Soon will the ships come home on the gales of morning,
Soon her lover's ship, and her tall brown lover,
The sailor-lad, soft-spoken, who is hers.
And he will smile to her his secret smile,
Tending the tiller as the boat swings past,
And wave to her as if to all he waved,
And meet her eyes with his, then look away.
Her lids are lowered and her lips just smile,

For she is conjuring in dream those eyes —
Bitter and bright and blue,
Like thin-topped waves against the sun,
The eyes men fear —
But she knows they can warm and seem to touch
Resistlessly.

And all the while she hums forgetfully
An old, old song the Breton girls have sung
Since first they loved and feared
And eased their hearts in song
(Perhaps Iseult of Brittany
Was humming the same words in that same place
A thousand years ago,
What time she waited for Lord Tristan
Whom she loved so grievously):

> *My only love is a sailor lad*
>   *Whose home is the fickle sea.*
> *To other girls he gives his smiles,*
>   *But his mouth he gives to me.*

> *On Sunday morning after mass*
>   *When he is dressed so fine,*
> *He stops before their open doors,*
>   *But at night he comes to mine.*

> *O Mary, bless all sailor lads*
>   *Whose loves are two and three,*
> *But mine keep safe from other girls —*
>   *Or let him die in the sea!*

And as the last line leaves her lips
She pauses, puckers up her mild girl's brow,
Then laughs a low contented laugh,
And sings again, half crooningly.
But summer sunshine, jubilant with cock-crows,
Is rattling open all the shuttered town.
The cross-roads gild, and housewives with their mops
Splash on the family door-step; street by street
Hears emptily the melancholy calls,
Reiterant and shrill, of country women,
Shoving their push-carts full of salad leaves
And gasping fish and lentils, frosty green.
Soon shore and beach and jetty are swarming and laughing
With fishermen's wives and mothers
And fathers and children and friends,
Come down to welcome the fleet:
Old men with cautious, simple eyes
And polished wrinkles carved in wood,
Old women coiffed in white
With wide clean aprons, baskets on their arms,
And little boys with windy looks and sober ways,
Breeched and jumpered in mandarin sail-cloth —
All shuffling in wooden shoes
That clatter and thump on the cobbles —
And the girl at the end of the jetty
Among them and of them,
Laughing the laughter that hides.
At last the black line of the wind appears,
Dragging behind unevenly the fleet.
And instantly the shore is ruffled
With ant-hill runnings up and down,

And pointing hands and voluble, unheeded chatter.
But she is silent,
Clutching her shawl in the freshening breeze,
And pale — or pale as peasant girls may be —
For the fishing boats are returning
And the sailors return from the sea.
Moth after moth, gold-winged on the golden morning,
Bursting and drinking the light green spray of the tide,
They fly with flashing and splendor out of the ocean,
Straining for waters of calm and the haven they know.
As each ship rounds the mole with sail careening
The girl leans out,
Searching the weathered faces of the crew.
And now her lover's boat flings past,
Wrapped in a dazzle of spray, dripping with brine,
Tilting its saffron sail in the rainbow wash
As it shoulders the mole.
Ah, the girl is a pendent flower!
Her mouth, her eyes, her soul,
Above him, gazing, waiting!
But he, forgetful, wrangles with the ropes,
And never lifts his head, nor waves his hand,
Nor sends one smile
Up to her eager face.
And the last late boat comes home,
And the fishing's done,
And hulls are emptied of their freight —
Mauve and silver-scaled sardines —
And sails are furled
And in the quiet sunlight from the masts
The nets are hung to dry —

The sea-soaked azure nets,
Bluer than filaments of unflawed turquoise.
But the girl alone on the bright deserted jetty
Still stands in the staring sunshine,
Her warm breast leaned against the spray-damp coping
It leaned more warmly on when he passed by.
But now her head is crouched behind her arms,
Her shawl clutched to her mouth,
And out across the hazing sea her wide eyes stare
Unseeingly and full of fear.

And the ancient wind from Tristan's isle comes sighing,
From the isle where long ago
Iseult with white hands folded on her lap,
Night after night,
Before the smouldering faggot fire,
Sat watching for some little tenderness
From Tristan,
Tristan the knight, whose heart to Cornwall clave
Unpityingly,
As all men know.

PART III
ENZIO'S KINGDOM, AND OTHER POEMS

II
DELTA SKETCHES

IN THE DELTA

The river country's wide and flat
    And blurred ash-blue with sun,
And there all work is dreams come true.
    All dreams are work begun.

The silted river made for us
    The black and mellow soil
And taught us as we conquered him
    Courage and faith and toil.

The river town that water oaks
    And myrtles hide and bless
Has broken every law except
    The law of kindliness.

And north and south and east the fields
    Of cotton close it round,
Where golden billows of the sun
    Break with no shade or sound.

Dear is the town, but in the fields
    A little house could be,
If built with care and auspices,
    A heart's felicity.

O friend, who love not much indoors
    Or lamp-lit, peopled ways,
What of a field and house to pass
    Our residue of days?

We'd learn of fret and labor there
    A patience that we miss
And be content content to be
    Nor wish nor hope for bliss.

With the immense untrammelled sun
    For brother in the fields,
And every night the stars' crusade
    Flashing to us their shields,

We'd meet, perhaps, some dusk as we
    Turned home to well-earned rest,
Unhurried Wisdom, tender-eyed,
    A pilgrim and our guest.

GREENVILLE TREES

THE LOMBARDY POPLARS:

Captive in this drab alien land,
We dreamed of all the great and wise
Who took the roads our shadows spanned
With song on lips and sword on thighs.

King Richard fared, one morn of May,
Our leafy lane to Palestine
With Blondel following. Well-a-day,
They sang of God and love and wine!

We leaned to pity once that girl
Who left the Loire one dripping spring,
So red of mouth, so brown of curl,
To be love's slave and Scotland's king.

Crusaders, knights, and troubadours
Rode through our golden-panelled shade:
We never thought these songless shores
Could rival that dead cavalcade.

But, petulant of simple joys,
Loving Death's mother, blind Romance,
We watched the passionate Delta boys
Stride down the street that leads to France.

THE CHINA-BERRIES:

Thousands of years ago,
We were weaving in moonlit Manchu gardens
Webs and arabesques of purple
On the moon-gray pebbled paths
For slender empresses,
In silver, lavender, and rose,
To tread on with their fuchsia-tinted sandals.
And one, on such a night,
Paused in our falling veils of subtle fragrance
And lifted up her arms
To the weary, much-prayed-to moon,
And wept for love.
But we have never seen these pale new people
Lift their arms to the exquisite moon
Or linger in our perfume.
They seem unconscious
Of the marvel of our blossoms,
Our stamens purpler-black than clematis,
Our delicate wisteria-tinged corolla.
Yet slender-fingered undulant princesses
Have bit their coral lips
And slain in anger
Prostrate imperial attendants
Because no loom could match our secret dyes.

Here we must tolerate small girls
With strange, sun-colored hair
Who thread our blossoms

And loop them with coarse clover-chains
About their throats.
Or worse, near summer-time,
Small boys, with eyes that have no darkness,
Will clamber into our branches,
Wounding our tender bark of satin,
Snapping our wonderful patterned leaves,
And pull our berries,
Hard, green, with infinitesimal speckles;
Then filling our indignant shade with laughter,
Jolly, uncouth, immoderate,
Mash them into their popguns
And frighten the sparrows even
And the reverent ancient negroes
With their insolent bombardment. . . .

Only the winter robins love us,
And then our boughs are naked,
And our shrivelled berries
Hang down in milky yellow clusters,
Fingered by faded winds,
Against a gray interminable sky.
Yet then too we are beautiful!

THE LOCUSTS:

In vain we fill the winter's palms
With rush of round, thin, golden alms.
The winter has no care for us
But breaks our brittle branches thus,
        Abjuring calms.

Yet one week of the year is ours:
We sun our creamy, scented flowers
And madden all the town. Oh, they
Are powerless, though prim, to stay
          Our fragrant powers.

The crowded church we bloom before
Leaves carelessly an open door:
Young sinners' eyes desert their books
And meet with long-lashed pagan looks
          And read no more.

Ah, watch for them, when shadows wait,
Walking the levee, slow, sedate!
But blush to guess the darling sights
When perfumes are the only lights,
          And it grows late.

THE WATER OAKS:

Once in our branches
Swarms of green parrakeets in seething turmoil settled,
Chattering north from the sweltering rank pampas,
Clothing us doubly in delightful leaves,
And suddenly departing.
But long ago, one violet spring,
We watched their wavering throngs melt down the south
To come again no more. . . .
We have been darkened by clouds of pigeons
Weltering like a cyclone
Across the watery rose sunset.

But some great death
Slew them: they come no more. . . .
More beautiful than all the wings that fly in beauty,
The wild swans,
Noble and full of fellowship,
Came in old days
Down the broad curves and brimming tremble of the river,
Or overland, at night, against the stars.
Oppressed with solemn joy
And ever-urgent purpose undisclosed,
They hovered in the twilight of cool autumn
Or mounted on the sunrise, trumpeting
And glad of rest, though brief.
For all their beauty
Each year we saw their glistening ranks dissolve,
Dissolve and waste, till now
Once in a winter and with pain
We spy perhaps a lone white wanderer,
Mateless and without friend,
Circling uncertainly and with hoarse piteous cries,
Till mercifully, with no thought of mercy,
The gray-eyed hunter on the river bars,
Making of murder sport, deprives
Him of his loneliness, the deep sky of a swan.
So too the races passed that lived beneath our leaves —
The patient, thought-pressed builders of the mounds
That came from mystery,
Returning whence they came;
The stealthy copper tribes
Whose arrows slit the blue beyond our heights,
Who, making moonlight haggard with their fires,

Danced in bad triumph at their brothers' death,
But in the end found never a cause to dance.
So too shall pass their pallid conquerors
Who now in slaying us have made the land
Naked and without loveliness of shade.
Though they have planted seed where once we towered
And hemmed the river's strength
And wedged us in their curveless hot-floored towns,
They too shall pass,
And we shall watch them die.

In the beginning there were three
And in the end there shall be only three:
The trees, the river,
And the outspread lonely tree of heaven,
Whose boughs are blossomy apple-wreaths at dawn,
Autumnal red and purple in the sunset,
And laden, night long, with the fruitage of the stars,
A harvest for some still-delaying husbandman.

THE HOLY WOMEN

    I have seen Mary at the cross
        And Mary at the tomb
And Mary weeping as she spread her hair
        In a leper's room.

    But it was not in Bethany
        Or groping up Calvary hill
I learned how women break their hearts to ease
        Another's ill.

    Compassionate and wise in pain,
        Most faithful in defeat,
The holy Marys I have watched and loved
        Live on our street.

A BURNISHED CALM

If I could be as calm as willow branches
When the sunlight turns them copper-pink and gold
And they lift their slender wands in the winter sunshine
From out the red-brown coffee-weeds into the blueness;
If I could know the calm of willow branches
When the hollows of the woods hold azure smoke
And the southern winter blurs and tarnishes;
If I could feel their passive unstrained certainty
As they wait the still-uneager, leaf-laden springtime,
Not fearing it will never come or come
Less beautiful, not doubting the return in time
Of downy buds and wrinkled burgeoning
And all the filmy lustre of warm days;
If I could be like willows by the river-bank in winter,
I think that wars remembered and presaged,
The drugging sense of doom and old disaster,
Would not oppress and strangle me as now.
But I should have a faith unflawed by these,
Discerning through the mad inclement now
The right's august recurrence in the race,
And like the leafless willows by the river
Wait in the winter sunshine trustfully
And with a burnished calm.

LEVEE NOCTURNE

A swan hangs brooding where the light
    Is colorless and cool —
Or is it but the moon above
    Her amethystine pool?

The powdered dusk is sifting down,
    The purple willows blur,
The air awaits its stars and bats
    And unseen moths that whir.

The houses light their lamps of gold
    Where bread is blessed and broken;
The noises of the day seem but
    A foolish word once spoken.

Only the quietness remains,
    So tender and so deep,
When the weary, weary pent-in-life
    Escape awhile in sleep.

A MEMORY

I saw four days of spring come floating down
Among the hard-gray lonely days of winter.
They came with full-blown warmth down the blue air
Like four pink petals shook from a loose wild rose
Or four pink clouds crossing an April sunrise
Or four young pilgrims stoled in misty rose,
Smelling of musk and with an Eastern grace.
And as they fell, softly, one after one,
On the shrivelled earth, delight returned, long absent:
The single trees in the fields, the many trees
In the woods, wrapped them in webs of rainbow gauze;
Lads dreamed of braided tresses, and the breeze
Of clear, clear water falling in pure sunlight;
Violets came, the purple and the gray
Wild sort that flaunt themselves and have no smell;
The jonquils trooped out in their sky-gold dresses,
Nodding and whispering like girls from school;
The great oaks seemed a haze the breeze might scatter,
Though blackbirds creaked and coughed on every bough;
The weeping willows, amber gales at anchor,
Danced in the rhythm of spring waterfalls;
And there was wistfulness and joy four days and nights.
Then came the frost:
The wizened buds lay speckled on the ground,
Winter came back, more bitter for its going.
Four days of spring and of a spring long past!
You ask me why I should remember them?

If you had ever loved and been beloved,
Even so briefly as four days and nights,
You would remember many things perhaps
That now I think you do not even see.

SONG

Sorrowful leaves of the winter oak
That cannot fall and cannot flutter,
Clutching, with love too deep to utter,
The branches that loved you when green was
   your cloak —
Fall, fall, for your green is gone,
And none loves love for itself alone,
And a faithful lover's a worrisome thing
In the spring, the spring, the tender spring.

OUTCAST

A summer's twilight ramble brought me where
I too shall sleep, if prayers are answered still.
No sad particular errand led me there,
But thoughts I let, that evening, have their will.

The graves are very quiet in that light,
Simple, despite their angels and their urns;
"Asleep in Jesus," "Rest in Peace," the trite
Poor epitaphs, seem then the due one earns.

Each bore its name and date, and so appealed
To cherish what already was forgot;
Some still could boast of wreaths, some, hardly healed,
Of wilted flowers and a mown grass-plot.

I passed with half a smile and half a sigh,
And came to those wild grasses where they too,
With no rememberer to tend them, lie
With equal peace in hammocked rags of dew.

I found there, by a purple iron-weed
Hung with black beetles, one lone slab that bore
No name, no date, but only this strange screed:
"Nature, who played the trick, can laugh no more."

Whether that outcast grave was tenanted
Or waits for one still walking earth's wide floor
I knew not, yet in fear I stooped and read:
"Nature, who played the trick, can laugh no more."

THE DELTA AUTUMN

Give me an ebbing sunset of the fall
With chilly flare of cosmos-colored light,
A white-winged moon in frozen, downward flight,
Ethereal, naked trees where no birds call;
Leave me to watch my infinite, gaunt river,
Its solemn width, its willow-purpled coil,
Its floor of hammered brass and azure oil,
Its silence where far strands of wild geese quiver —
And I'll not miss the hopeful, passionate spring,
Spring that knows naught of thought or masterful will
Or conquered grief or peace when cold winds chill,
But sings and struts with sunlight-dabbled wing
And is too sweet where men yet hate and kill.
Autumn as autumn comes in my dim-lustered land —
Of that be my dreaming under the fennel-crusted sand.

PART III
ENZIO'S KINGDOM, AND OTHER POEMS

III
A LETTER FROM JOHN KEATS TO FANNY BRAWNE

A LETTER FROM JOHN KEATS
TO FANNY BRAWNE

Rome, December, 1820

I had not thought to ever taste again
The mellowness of living. But today
The fever's less, the creeping end is only
A warm tide of luxurious weariness
And steady, rich discernment, rare of late.
This mild Italian autumn of tarnished leaves,
The sunshine thick like yellow muscadel
With nectarous smell of overripe bruised fruits,
The autumn feel of pause, accomplishment,
Finality almost, and tears behind,
Have so infected me with their serene
That I experience wisdom without wisdom's pain. . . .
I can recall such hours before we met,
But none or few thereafter. . . . No, that's not true:
No wisdom calmed my days before we met;
Their best was heartless crystalline delight,
Such as a bird must feel mounting the sunrise;
While this mood in its peace seems posthumous,
The spent year's spell, in which I see my life
And all our love rounded and closed like music. . . .
Now in a day or two, at most a month,
I shall be sleeping in a dreamy place
Where Severn says the springtime is wet blue
With violets and smoothest red and white

With cool camellias, fit for tapestry.
You must not worry. 'Twill be a quiet sleeping
Under this sky, so beautiful, yet not
The sky of home. . . . Before that dull time comes
I must unvenom all my old reproaches
And tell you how, gauging the whole strange tale
Of our sweet love, I find there only comfort —
No anguish, no regret — and in my heart
Nothing of love except love's tenderness.

I thought, I tried to think, my suffering
Was passion's unfulfilment, the divorce
Of you and me by poverty, disease.
But now I know — I always knew, I think —
The cause was simpler and incurable.
That I have suffered from this love of ours
You know too well for me in kindness now
To half gainsay. But you could never know
How much your hand at rest on Brown's firm shoulder
Above my invalid's chair could torture me;
Or how, when your so longed-for letters came —
That never said enough — I had no strength
To open them, but covered them with kisses,
Like any scullery maid, and broke the seal
Each time with all the dreadful pang of heartbreak.
Ah, pain enough, dear girl, and pain to spare,
But through no fault of yours, for you are faultless!
At last I dare to recognize the cause
Of why I found love like a bloody sweat:
You could not love me but in your own way,
And that — that was a way that was not mine.

I had known much of grief, too much of death,
And never been the comrade of good fortune;
My passion had no lightness and no grace,
It burned me up — a death pyre by the sea
At night, its red light putting out the stars.
There was no moment of the day or night
I did not hunger for you. I saw your face,
Your throat, your hair, more real, more tangible
Than anything within my true eyes' vision;
Your rare low words of love, your thoughtless laughter,
Haunted my hearing like a song remembered. . . .
I cannot think what my love meeting love
As fearful as itself had ended in!
Yours was the love it met, and so that thought
Is speculative. . . . Yours was the love, my dearest,
And you were just eighteen — not Guinevere,
Francesca, or Iseult, but merely Fanny —
If less than they in majesty of mind,
Their equal in the accident of beauty.
How could I hope that I could be to you
The rudiment and base of happiness,
The dovecote of all thoughts, the fold of dreams,
The desert fountain, as you were to me?
Who had expected, if the fragrant Psyche
Had fled from Greece and turned an English girl,
That she should mourn all day the missing Eros
And not be friendly with the English boys,
Touching their hands and dancing in their dances,
Laughing with them, untroubled by her love?
It was too much to hope that you should sicken
Because love wounded me. You loved me — yes —

And were as kind as mothers to their children.
But, oh, you loved me with a girl's light love,
And could have loved as easily another!
That was the unslaked thirsting of my life
And that the poisoned knowledge I abhorred. . . .
You see how gentleness was difficult
And why ofttimes I blamed you without cause,
Conceding not at all that you and I
Were made to hurt each other, being made
By different gods, in different moods, removed
By nature and conjoined by cynic chance.

That's past; forget with me its bitterness,
Remembering instead that out of this
Impossible, precipitous, starved love
Came all that I may claim of worth and beauty —
(I'd like to think you'd care to read these words
Slowly and more than once, they mean so much) —
You, who took all I had, gave all I have.
You were not wholly Madeleine, perhaps,
Nor even that Belle Dame who wrought such woe,
But had your loveliness not pierced my soul
And stolen my peace and made me friend of anguish,
I should have written in their stead, no doubt,
Another and as poor Endymion.
Even the nightingale was poignant by
Your absence, and lacking you I learned of her
Her secret, and found me shelter from love's cold
In beauty's house. . . . My glistening perfect garlands,
Woven of ilex dark and polished bay,
Should not in justice lie across the threshold

Of that high temple of the god of song,
But on your doorstep, like a sweetheart's posy.
Then, too, love brings with his fine cruelty
Such fellowship of tears and sense of sorrow!
Without you I was intimate with gods
And sylvan deities and fairy folk,
Wept at romances in a dog-eared book,
And found a song more moving than live pain.
But these last days, with all my singing stopped,
I am amazed to find stored up in me
Compassion's very substance and a glow
Of human pity never dreamed before.
I see my kinship with the dreadful world
And, healed of youthful blindness, recognize
The brotherhood of grief. There is no warmth
Of poesy or bliss so purged and fierce
As this that laves about my naked heart
Since I have made discovery of man.
I watch them from my window here at Rome,
And not a face but tells beneath its masque
Of some such commonplace as death or fear
Or passion starved or passion fed to grossness.
And in the night when Severn thinks I sleep
I watch the pale processional stream past —
Humanity, like wounded from a battle.
Oh, all the eyes quenched out that once were stars!
Oh, all the lips that sag and blench with pain!
Eternal loneliness in search of love!
I know their secret, taste their hidden tears,
And, one of them, to each one stretch my arms. . . .
Aged twenty-four! And as I'm leaving it

I understand the world — because of you!
Shakespeare, you know, had fifty years or more,
Yet I could talk with him and not feel young.
Well, I'll not keep you longer reading words
That may or may not have a meaning in them.
Severn (who should be friendship's synonym
And lacks in nothing but a woman's touch)
Will soon be running up the stairs and stand
Aghast to find me wasting thus my strength.
When I have calmed him I shall beg for those
Light-hearted and ethereal filigrees
Haydn and Mozart made of silver sound.
They cool me . . . almost as much as one cool hand
That used to stroke my forehead. Oh, not yet,
Not yet, ask me to write the last farewell!
I wish it could be just one breathed caress,
Lingering, like a prayer, and unlike those
You were familiar with and maybe loved.
O Fanny, how I long for you to fathom
All, all the tenderness and thanks I feel,
Here turning in the doorway of dumb death,
For you. You are so far away and lonely!
I see you as the wistfulest thing alive,
So young and unadvised and full of joy,
Irrevocably travelling down the years
To meet irrevocable dark misfortune,
With beauty for your weak and sole defense
And lust of living for your only guide.
Not to be close where you could call to me,
Not to lean over you when tears must come
And you be trampled by the brutal world —

There's the one last regret that dying has! . . .
Someone will take my place in that respect. . . .
I will not say I envy him — O God —
But that I wish him some such gentleness
As mine, and power to protect far greater. . . .
Do not remember me if memory hurts.
Good-bye, bright star, good-bye. God bless you, Fanny.

PART III

ENZIO'S KINGDOM, AND OTHER POEMS

IV

ENZIO'S KINGDOM

ENZIO'S KINGDOM

Dead, then, the most imperial of emperors
And by some accident of flesh my father!
I am content, Berard; nay, I am glad.
Life's infamy was overgalling to him.
He suffered like a god that had no part
In its creation, but was resolved — how madly —
To make it over, if not beautiful,
Tolerable at least and roomed for men.
And then, Berard, his godlike loneliness
With only you and me to lean upon!
I but a gold-haired bastard lad and you
An old man sworn to serve the Church he loathed,
Forsworn for love of him; and both of us
Brimmed and surbrimmed by his enormous dreams
And alchemized in his fond fiery love —
But of ourselves unmeriting and common.
How could all nature not rise up and be
His partisan? How could he fail, Berard,
Unless the very dastard race of men
He suffered for deserve its doom of failure?

But I forget the laws of courtesy,
Remembered first, and last forgot by him.
The night is late and you have travelled far
And secretly to tell me of his death.
I should say words of thanks and let you go.
Your hand shakes and you have great need of sleep —

We both have need of sleep, I think — long sleep.
But O, Berard, when that door clangs behind you
It will not ever open on a friend;
And I, the young king of Sardinia,
The emperor's son, will be a tame pet prisoner
Till the end, till the long sleep we need so.
Sit down, I pray you: let me talk of him —
Of him they call the Second Frederick,
But I call father. Tears — ah! And in your eyes.
How many times I've wept so at your knee!

You knew him from his birth, as you knew me,
For which I have it in my heart to envy you.
I've often wondered of that little boy
With red wild hair and sultry shadowed eyes,
Orphaned and penniless, the old Pope's ward,
An unwished, scanted guest from house to house
Among the ignorant burghers of Palermo —
Despite which the incorrigible heir
Of Barbarossa's and blond Guiscard's blood.
Those years of vile neglect and unjust anguish
Were often in his eyes, when fixed on me,
And made, I think, the passionate tenderness
Of his solicitude and vigilant love.
I was to be all he had never been —
The darling citizen of his new world;
Delight's own bosom friend; above all, free.
Now he is dead, his rosy world salt red,
And I the citizen of four wet walls,
Of freedom and of father both bereft!
If he had been content to merely be

The Kingdom's king, the lord of Sicily:
If when great Barbarossa's heavy crown
Was tendered to his brows uncrowned with manhood
He had refused it, had not dashed with you
And that gay handful of adventurers
To Constance, crashed the gates to, laughed at Otho —
Today he might be hawking in the Kingdom,
Or matching rhymes with young-voiced troubadours,
Or naming stars with some lean Arab seer:
And I'd be hearing still his great clean laugh.
But then he had been an oblivion's king,
Not Frederick, the Wonder of the World,
The Torch shook out one great amazed short instant,
Then dashed, to leave for us intenser dark. . . .

Within this nothingness ahead, I'll try
Forgetting of the smoky latter years,
The blood spilled and the failure, and solace me
With dreaming of his dream when it was true —
At least it seemed so once in our Palermo.
'Tis not the rich deceptive blue of retrospect
Makes so serenely excellent those days
When you and I, Pietro and Thaddeus,
Were cornerstones of his imperial life,
Miraculously graven with his love.
There never was on earth such dowered peace,
Such laughter blowing through old wisdom's cell,
Such intellect shot like a proud gold arrow
Into the giant freedom of the sun!
Mere memory of those times is more alive
Than the brash breathing days allowed most mortals!

That room, Berard, that opened on the sea,
Full of slant sunbeams in the afternoon,
Where he revised the idiot world's affairs
With you by as grave councillor and me,
No taller than a broadsword, listening,
Quite gravely too, as like as not my head
Against his knee, beneath his hovering hand —
That room touched with its inmate light the lengths
Of Araby, Illyria, England, Greece,
Dazzled outlandish folk beyond the Rhine,
Warmed Aragon, Provence, dull Austria,
And flared our own obscure sweet Sicily
Into the day-star of a starless night.
I'd listen in a blinking glow of wonder
To orders, laws, decisions, policies:
A fleet to Reggio; a thousand men to Jaffa;
A brace of falcons to the king of France;
To our belovèd vassals of Cologne
A charter and the right of toll; requests
For cotton and the barley seed he promised
Of Sultan Kamel, our especial friend,
Appended to a note on Aristotle;
Exemption of all silk looms from taxation;
Death for a judge whose greed was not for justice;
Appointment of a notary for Flanders,
A seneschal for Treves, a captain for
The ships of oil and wheat outbound for India;
Our thanks to Brother Leo for the copy
Of that last Canticle as Francis wrote it,
Enclosing our own manuscript on hawking;
An edict granting freedom to the Jews:

The whole a brave clear text of liberal wisdom
Illumined with light-hearted blue and gold!
The pageant of the world passed through that room,
Their colors burning in the moted sunlight —
Ambassadors and pilgrims, knights and seers,
Star-gazers, troubadours, philosophers,
The wise, the wisdom-seeking, the renowned.
The race's best and foremost swarmed to him
As night-things to a streaming far-seen light.

But when the day was over, the candles lit,
The last petitioner gone, the empire's needs
Dismissed till morning, then it was, Berard,
The day began, for then we were alone.
He'd think aloud to me, pacing the room's length
Or standing mute, one hand lost in his beard,
His brain the battle-ground of two strong thoughts.
'Twas then the infinite details of his task
Assembled in perspective, and resolved
To fractions of his intricate patterned dream.
And when his vehement revery was done
That smile he had for me would quite uncloud
His face, and with one arm about my shoulder
He'd pass out to the sea-cooled balcony
Where the full darkness fell and no sound stole.
And he would stand there silent a long while,
Watching in a profound remote repose
The multitudinous slow flight of stars,
All hush and ecstasy, or, far beneath,
The bleak silver ocean barred with black,
Calm as eternity, though quivering always.

Then he would say: " Now let us sleep, my son.
The infinitudes of beauty with no toil
Pursue their ministries we may not guess,
Though vibrant to the music they exhale:
Our waking or our sleep will vex them not."
He was aware no keenlier of the actual
Than of the instigating powers that buoy us.
Caesar, I think, nor Alexander saw
So rightly nor so far into the dark.

The day that thrust me suddenly from boy's
To man's estate shines yet through fifteen years.
It was the day he honored Michael Scott
As though the king of India were his guest,
Not some pinched nobody in broidered gown
Of stars and moons and suns and hieroglyphs,
Who dubbed himself astrologer and watched
Dancing girls, rabbis, princes, desert sheiks —
The palace-full assembled in his honor —
In the cold English way and never laughed.
But most, I found, he watched my glowing father,
Single in debonair and gracious ease
Among the guests. And I could swear, Berard,
There was some dry and cynic pity in his gaze.
Then Pietro asked him, in a voice all heard,
What was the emperor's own fated star.
With his thin smile and pale satiric eyes
He answered in a blight of sudden silence
" Canopus," and again the silence closed.
My father's laugh was shorter than his words:
" A star so small his very name's unknown."

"Ask of your Arab friends," the wizard's voice
Ran smooth as ice: "In fiery magnitude
He is the greatest of all stars." "Then why,"
Pursued my father, "should I have never seen
His flaming orb?" There was a long strange pause.
At last the answer came, but hardly heard:
"He is too bright for our cold northern skies.
They see him but an instant, then he goes."
My father laughed, "Thanks for a brilliant moment,"
And with accustomed calm and showered banter
Passed through the company. Alone with me,
In silence that seemed almost sorrowful,
He reached the room I loved and sat awhile
In some abstracted lassitude of thought,
While I, boylike, wished Michael Scott were dead.
Thus da Vigna found us.

    O even now
'Tis hard to hate da Vigna — and then he seemed
The perfect knight; as poet, councillor,
Vice-regent, friend, the nonpareil and pattern.
There was such glitter of resolve about him,
Such frankness, yet such reticence of mood,
As if he were a quarrying hawk that hovered
For game far off before he flashed and struck.
Ah, well, that night he only came to reckon
What stallions would be needed for Apulia,
And how Phoenician trade might be drawn off
From Genoa and the purple ships of Venice.
Pietro da Vigna leaned across the table
Fingering maps and schedules while my father,

Sunk in his cushioned chair almost a throne,
Listened, the weavings of his burnished gown
Seeming to breathe in the gold-spun candlelight.
Then Pietro said the rebel town of Bari —
To capture which was his express stout task —
Had not yet fallen, nay, it would not fall
Until a further complement of men
Was furnished them that had attacked in vain.
There was a panther stir in the great chair.
" I have no men to send you," came his voice.
" Then Bari holds out till the crack o' doom,"
Broke bitterly from Pietro. My father grew
Stone still, and when his voice at last whipped out
It was no friendly voice: " Why ask for men
Before you have exhausted gold and guile? "
Da Vigna's hand went dead among his papers
And dead his face, except his eyes that winced.
But he was silent. Again the emperor spoke:
" Bribe them: or feast their leaders at a truce
And poison them." Pietro at that leaped up,
Pale truly, but a thousand miles from fear:
" Bribe or assassinate, your Majesty,
But find a fitter tool for such base work."
His voice was steady challenge and despair.
I shut my eyes so that I might not see
My father's terrible anger boiling up,
But when I looked his chin was on his hand
And he regarded Pietro dreamily
And from a cold great distance. Then he said,
As if in weariness: " Sit down: compose
That answer to the Pope we planned together,

While I have Enzio read aloud to me
His last translation from the happy Greek.
His Arab master found it in Byzantium."
So, gulping down the terror I had felt,
I found the manuscript, leaned back against
His knees, and while da Vigna seemed to write
And he to sleep, for he was breathless-still,
With eyelids closed, I read aloud to him.
And the very candles seemed to fall asleep.

It was the story of the son of Helios,
His gold-haired only son, not yet a man,
Who, watching his divinely sinewed father
Drive from the stables of the dark each dawn
The chariot and horses of the sun,
Besought that he might be their driver once
And for one glorying lonely day race up
The azure mountain of the infinite air.
And dotingly his father gave him leave,
While his young sisters of the clear gold hair
Wept for him as they wandered by the river
Gathering hyacinths. But who may bear
The burden of all light through solitude
Except a god? Or, swathed in dizzy foam
Of hissing manes, hold to their difficult course
Those passionate stallions fed on naked fire?
Half up the sky, seething in whirlwind light,
He gazed in anguish on the earth he knew,
The friendly, populous earth, dappled with shade,
And through his sweat-bright hands the taut reins slipped.
Down plunged the horses, down the chariot plunged;

And like a meteor in full day descried
Headlong the gold-haired son of Helios fell —
Silent and lovely, his hand before his eyes. . . .
I ceased. There was great quietness, except
My father's hand was groping in my hair.
It seemed he had been speaking ere he spoke:
" But thou shalt never fall, my son, nor guide
Alone the golden chariot of the sun.
My hands shall grasp the reins and close beside me
Thou shalt behold the turmoil of my sky,
The sweetness of thine earth, smiling, untroubled."

He rose and paced the floor his pauseful way
When brooding, and smouldered as he dreamed aloud:
" For mankind in the mass, truth is what works —
A creed, a fair illusion, a reward; —
Some worthy lie by which they shuffle through
In something that approaches happiness.
Not their content nor their accomplishment
Are for the few whose greed is truth itself.
Our desolate and ice-cold consolation
Is that no matter what the vacancy
Unstarred and horrible we stumble on
In the scheme of things, it cannot be as bleak
And choking and insufferable as this
All-drowning ignorance we welter in.
For us there are no terrors and few joys,
But only courage and a blown bright hope . . .
To grip the tatterdemalion unsorted world
And make a plan of it — that's our occupation:
Preëminently mine, who in the chaos

Am thrust as ruler, and recognize indeed
My own mind as a mountain among hills.
Were I an indolent dreamer I could weep
At all the tongues and all the arrogant creeds
Disharmonizing man, obscuring his
Essential unity and native likeness,
And wish in futile wrath to blot them out.
Instead, not futilely, I grapple facts;
And spite of races, tongues and creeds at odds
Impose the unity of my bold justice
Upon a turbulent world from Nazareth
To Ghent. . . . That is the ground-work of all
 peace. . . .
Peace. Peace. The great prerequisite,
The race's single chance to reach its stature . . .
There's not a lie too great, a crime too gross
I'll not be guilty of, if so thereby
I may establish it and fix the lines
Of the quivering vision I intend the world. . . .
Am I the first that with sheer intellect
Has hated war, not weeping at its woe
So much as raging at its waste and folly?
Let me be first: and by the stablishment
Of peace I'll show my elders' errancy. . . .
And after peace I shall enchant the world
Into a universal Sicily
And prove life even can be livable. . . .

" Protect the masses in their breeding moil;
Feed them; and sweeten them by fear's remove:
But do not build for them, for they are doomed

To everyday contents and grievances —
Unspeculative, level, themselves their study.
But, oh, the flashing-eyed minority,
The Enzios of the world, the sons of light —
These I would turn free-pinioned on an earth
That they would make august and radiant!
Think, think, O gods, what freedom could mean here,
Freedom to think and be and to pursue
The sovereign hope a stormy heart may spring!
Never have they been loosened from the toils
Of fear, and sin imagined, and old thoughts,
And ever at their elbows threatened priest
Or king or skeleton of fleshly want.
I'll change all this: and for imperial boon
Grant freedom to the spirits of the free.
Watch them: already they are homing to me,
And there's no man today not sworn my vassal
If Truth or High Endeavor be his liege.
So much to learn, forgot or never learned!
Such flight-room for the gold bird of the mind!
Such loveliness to build or paint or set
In colored words of leisure on a parchment!
Oh, I conceive a breathing-space, for men
Of vestured soul, grander than heaven; yea,
And possible, a point oft overlooked
In heavenly and terrestial dreams, I judge.
And what to hinder, save the allotted span
Some yokel with a home-made stave may skimp?
So far I've won: my laws establish justice,
Justice peace, and the young future teems
To Naples and Salerno where my schools

Are aids and urgers to the starrier way.
My present is a sunny sky: but clouds
Unquietly from two bad quarters stir
And grope to make one storm, a storm so vast
It will blind out the opulent, life-giving sun. . . .
The rabble Lombard cities; and the Pope . . .
Can these bring back the ancient dark despite me?
Never. Never. Yet they draw off my force,
Like unjust judges; traitors; rebel cities —
Details a friend could spare me by assuming —
And I must close with them in battle. First,
The cities — orgulous, pestilently brave,
The pack of them fanging and foaming each on each
Like rutting dogs, and with the minds, means,
Manners of dogs. At large they bait the world
To brawls and bickerings, costly and futile:
But chained are frenzied martyrs howling 'Freedom,'
A word they fight for, but a fact, God knows,
They neither put to use nor grant to others.
The cities first: blood wasted and much gold,
But victory, the atrocious north restrained
And muzzled into manners and address. . . .
Then, Rome. . . . A struggle to the death, I fear. . . .
The war 'twixt emperors and popes will reach
In me its apogee, for good or ill.
Not that inherent differences appear
In Gregory's gage flung down to Frederick
And Hildebrand's to Barbarossa, but
The princes of the church divine in me
A serpent wiser and more venomous
Than in my crusty and impetuous grandsire.

He had perspective and fine taste for power
But was in fact a simple, loyal Christian.
While I — I see the thing that calls itself
Christ's Church a noble detriment, a dream
Once valid, but in the dawning old and evil.
I will concede the masses to the Pope:
Their stultified obedience makes for peace.
But I'll not give my eaglets to his cage:
For them there shall be freedom if it takes
The very toppling down of Peter's throne. . . .

" How blistered is the earth with outpoured blood
Which on the ground has but a human look —
Not Christian, Jewish, or Mohammedan!
They slaughter each the other in the name
Of Allah, Christ, Jehovah, that one god
Who needs a name to be distinguishable.
And now in Albi they would further tear
Their Christian sect of Rome into another,
And later still another, and another,
Till down the centuries the jargon of
Their creeds will rile, I swear, sweet-tempered Heaven!
Three is enough! I join with Rome at Albi
To drown this heresy in good French blood.
Three is enough: yet not enough, I know. . . .
Jesus, Mahomet, Abraham — good men
Guessing! I read their words with reverence
And know that still the ultimate word's not written. . . .
When I have made my tablet of the laws
To guide the flight of my young Enzios,
' Thou shalt not ' shall be missing from its rubric.

Perhaps two words will make its decalogue:
' Courage: Unselfishness.' These two suffice.
Oh, all this cry of ' sin,' these acts forbidden,
Ruffle my gorge! The Christian sins if meat
Is eat on Friday; the Jew if any day
He eats of pork; the Prophet's follower
If anything on any day he eats
With Jew or Christian at his friendly table.
Fools, fools, and serious fools who die
For imbecilities diverse but equal!
With hortatives and childish talk of sin
They so have staled the cleanly natural air
That life stinks like a sick-room. Bah! their ' sin ' —
There is no taint save its own consequence
To any deed; and what is wise is good!
The centuries' experience of a deed's
Outcome and burthen aids our judgment of it
Before 'tis done, but is not sacrosanct
Or final. If men would but forget what not
To do, and fix their wills and uttermost minds
On what to do and do it — they'd breed the world
With loveliness and power beyond all guessing!
Virtue is energy directed wisely:
And sin is sloth. . . . How am I judged here, now,
By this religious and oppressive world?
All I have wrought for justice and for peace,
For beauty's burgeoning and joy's flower,
Are these emblazoned on a scroll of praise?
Hardly. But I am damned as heretic,
And worse — an irony for Kamel — lecher!
I am not chaste, and so I spoil for hell!

These priests that never do the deed, but dream of it
Till their minds are porous — foetid — maggot's meat —
They grieve for me, who feed the monster I
Am caged in decently, I hope, and keep
My mind robust and cold as mountain wind. . . .
They do not even see the pity of it. . . .
How mockingly are our sweet bodies made
In that the very pang and leap of love
Is circumstanced in filth and sorry loathing!
And how wit-cursed the incarnating force
That fashions the idiot with no more pain
And no less air of nature justified
Than when a stripling god like Enzio's born!
No empress was your mother, Enzio;
But you were not begot half-heartedly,
Betwixt a dream and a sleep, the sanctioned way.

" But these are incidentals of a life
I purpose to make frank and vigorous. . . .
' Courage, Unselfishness,' and the youth of the world
At my heels! One could not fail with these nor shrink.
Truth sleeps and has indeed its evil dreams,
But never dies. . . . The Lombard cities scotched
And Rome's pretensions clipped, defined, made harmless,
I'll set the world upon a singing path
And rank it king-star of the heavenly host!
Such wisdom waits to be uncovered, Enzio;
Such loveliness to be evoked! O gods,
The splendor, majesty, and joy of life
Have not been tapped, but only wait upon
The spirit's franchise that I burn to grant. . . .

The chariot of the sun has issued forth,
The reins are in my hands — no turning back,
No stumbling, Enzio, nor halt, until
The azure circuit's run and regally
We rest our steeds in that mysterions stall —
Death's purple-raftered house. . . . Yet men stand back —
Men that should know and love me — baulk at some item,
Some Bari thrust between me and my purpose,
Which is today in the great staggering world
The only godlike, all-inclusive scheme
Of hope and betterment. . . . Was Helios lonely? "

He ceased, as if a great bell's toning ceased,
Leaving a chaos of grand sound and trembling.
Before the din had died, Pietro was speaking,
As tall and quiet-burning as a candle:
" Imperial master, grant me leave to go."
" Whither? " my father answered out of dimness.
" To Bari, which shall fall before this moon
Has shed her horns." Oh, it was good to hear
The wind of my father's laughter lift the shadows:
" Petrus, wound me no more so bitterly!
When we have built the new Jerusalem
Your name shall indicate right well your rank."
And from that day I was a boy no longer,
But saw his need of me and took my place.

That was the time life should have ceased, Berard,
Still fresh and glistening and mountain-aired,
Its only apprehension change or ending!
It is so grievous living past the prime

And looking back for all one's glimpse of glamour.
Surely no god who ever had been young
Could have watched idly so much loveliness
Undone! A wise and passionate innocence
Spangled our lives and made each hour awake
Keep the cool filmy fragrance of first waking. . . .
That passed too quickly — quicklier being lovely.
Our south, the south he loved so, saw him in
Pale lightning glimpses only after that night.
The storm was sooner breaking that he'd thought,
And never ended. Rome and the Lombard cities
Loosened their hate your news alone could quell.
Berard, Berard, it seems we have been fighting
Since the beginning of things, and all the rest's
A plaguing dream! And why it was — or when —
Or why it could not cease and let us be —
I cannot now remember. . . . Thanks, old friend. . . .
A faintness — yes — it's gone — the memories came
Too thick. . . . No, no, you cannot leave me yet!
Sleep is more torturing than weariness!
Just then when my eyes closed I saw his eyes —
Smoky with pain and void of recognition!
They make sleep full of fear: I cannot meet them!
Forgive me . . . I am not often not a man . . .
I am quite well now. . . . Yes, the air . . . the damp.
My window's small — but boasts Aldebaran,
A long hour, late. He's quite the same, Berard,
As when you taught a little boy his name
And pointed to him hanging through the palm trees.
It's very friendly of him to be here. . . .
I almost slipped from prison yesterday.

That was before I knew . . . My evil luck
Was Absalom's: one strand of tell-tale hair
Showed from the wine-butt I was hiding in. . . .
For that attempt I'm being lessoned now
On bread and water — I who was once a king!
Do you remember my first day of battle —
Cased in my golden greaves and coat of mail,
Burnished and proud and brave as seventeen?
He called me then Aldebaran, the prince
Of stars, and was as proud as I, but not
As far, as very far, from doubting tears. . . .

I soldiered well for seventeen: that's something:
And something more that three years afterward
I was commander of the imperial armies.
At first it had the zest of sportsmanship
And when we'd meet to plan some new campaign
My heart would swell to know myself his helper.
The best was when we thwarted Gregory.
That was my plan, Berard. To keep the Pope
From holding his great Conclave of the Church,
Or so much of it as was hostile to us,
Seemed of prime urgency, for, once assembled,
We had some glimmering of the onerous outcome.
My father had already sent his letter
To all the Christian kings of Christendom
Protesting 'gainst the Conclave's convocation.
How he and Pietro crackled at its making —
Its scriptural, grandiose air of indignation,
With just enough of formal reverence
To make them swallow down the new wild yeast

Of his rebellious and irreverent scorn.
And when they nominated Gregory
"The Beast with Horns" — and sternly — how we laughed!
It smacked of that audacious mad crusade
He undertook in jest or scorn or malice
And rounded to a cynical success
With wheat and oil and Kamel's tolerant friendship.
Yet in these scornful pranks one could detect
A calculated and subversive purpose:
To mock an idol without retribution
Will jar somewhat the best idolater.
Indeed, I thing his mockery's work will last
When much far nobler will have been forgot.
But the letter, though it jarred the Christian kings,
Did not prevent the Conclave's call to Rome.
So, as our armies domineered all roads
Converging on the imperial city north
And south, leaving their sole approach by sea,
I offered, half as humorous solution,
To catch the Conclave as it paddled past,
Reeking of lauds and incense, but convoyed
Stoutly enough by the whole fleet of Genoa;
Which done, we'd drop that freightage of old bones —
Three hundred cardinals, archbishops, what-nots —
Into some wholesome dungeon, while the Pope
Would rant and fall to scribbling bulls and banns
At the empty council table. Here was a jest
Fateful, adventurous, that took my father:
Da Vigna too was hopeful: you were absent.
So we devised how I should take the fleet
Of Pisa with what tonnage of our own

I could lay hands to, and strike the Genoese
While sailing down the mainland to the Tiber.
But I remember as our parley ended
My father's ardor wavered and went out,
And he was moody till we were alone.
Then as I turned to leave him he inquired,
" Have you no fear, no secret fear, my son,
Of Rome's much-feared and hard anathema
That falls on you now as it fell on me? "
But all that I could think to answer was,
" I am your son." He gripped me hard at that.
There is some balm in lingering on such moments
When he was proud my bastard blood was his. . . .
Another one was when I dashed from Pisa,
Riding in lathered haste, my tidings' own
Glad messenger. Ah, then time's brutal hand
Had not yet brushed the moth-gold from my youth!
Dusty and hollow-eyed and streaked with sweat
I burst upon him with the victory:
Our sally in the dark; the shock at dawn;
How such and such a ship was sunk or boarded;
Where sprang their main resistance, and its toll;
And who their worships were we clapped in prison.
I saved the humor of it for the last.
Archbishop though you are, you too had laughed
At those two prelates pigeon-paunched, red-gilled,
Who started excommunicating me
Right in the face of my own gaping troops.
My father ruffled when I told him of it.
But when I added with what unconcern
I cut in on their curse and whisked them off,

Blowsy with rage, to learn civility
And Christian meekness in a lousy cell —
He laughed till tears were shaking in his beard.
Then a great banquet, jousts and glees and tourneys —
And I the target of his toasts and praises.

There was not much of laughing loud together,
Or banqueting, after the Pisan coup.
Campaigns and sieges, battles and assaults —
Ungilding in the glut and mire of war.
We thought when Gregory died there would be respite,
But wished him back before this Innocent
Had run one scale upon his harp of hate.
He'll likely die now, when his death's no profit.
The evil always die too late for thanks,
Serene and impotent, their worst full blown.
I hated war, but matched against my father's,
My hatred of it was intemperate love.
There never was so great a warrior,
A general so visioned and aggressive,
Who so rebelliously despised his calling.
It wore into his very strength and sinews
Like trace-chains on the haunches of a charger.
But still his camp outlustered any court,
Was rumored into fable as the home
Of every undared dark delirious vice,
And still he browbeat fame and looked the victor. . . .
It was a specious semblance of his world.

When Innocent fled Rome for France, it seemed
Our victory, but was our brink of ruin.

There was no fleet to summon merrily
And catch the Conclave he convened for Lyons,
He did not fall in Gregory's trap. And I
Nor Pietro could devise a scheme to stave
The darkening fate that gathered as we gazed
To hurtle on a head so undeserving.
If he had gone himself, Berard, and stood
Before them in his cloak of burning wrath,
Could they have found him guilty? Oh, I think
They would have swept their croziers up like swords
And sworn to follow him, though bound for hell.
But likely not. They were old tepid men,
By whom to be adjudged as by one's equals
Was desecration and indignity.
So Thaddeus went, and Pietro followed him,
To act the absent and imperial
Protagonist; while one old man and I
With sombre hearts kept near the emperor
And made Turin our waiting place for news.

The tricks of prison life are strange, Berard.
Here in my cell I've paced so many times
That length of hall where his great feast was held
That I can count the casements down one wall,
The lolling torches sconced along the other,
And often, sleepless, in a mad calm dream
I seem to move about there in the moonlight,
Lonesome as Abel's ghost alone in death,
Searching for something missed but unremembered,
And gazing with vague misty eyes far out
Across the night-washed lowlands of Turin.

Why did he choose of all times that for feasting,
Summoning friends, near friends, near enemies,
To drink deep and to make a show of pleasure,
When all the while our hearts were raw with waiting
For news of Thaddeus and his mission's end?
But the room glittered with its crush of guests,
The dipping torch-light through its own blue smoke
Crimsoning carcanets and jewelled clasps,
Daubing with fire the burnished bowls and beakers —
And he too glittered from his daïsed throne
At the long table's end, above the crowd,
Superb in tissued gold and rash abandon.
How wearily for us the mirth rushed on!
And when we heard those clattering hoofs outside
Dash up and halt, how well we knew some fate
With hooded vizor stood, a wall's width from us,
And would not stand there long. So Thaddeus entered —
Forgive my telling what you know already!
I am a draft of visions. Hear me out,
Or I shall strangle in their mounting fumes! —
It seemed he'd never walk that length of room
And stand before my father, whispering.
Then lacked the emperor courtesy, if ever:
He brushed the words back Thaddeus was speaking
And rose; the chatter froze away to silence.
His own words sprang across the air like arrows:
" My friends, we have somewhat of news to hear
Which Thaddeus brings still piping from the Pope.
We'll hear it with you. The worst is not too bad
To share with friends, simply, with no concealment.
Speak, Thaddeus, speak: as if to me alone."

And Thaddeus faced us, anguish on his face
And such nobility as heartbreak chisels.

They could find naught wherewith to charge my father
Save heresy — no vileness, no one act
Infamous or diseased with evil outcome!
But day by day they clustered in their church,
Stinking with sweat and incense, and pawed through
The jewelled details of his passionate life,
Seeking for filth, hungry for carrion —
Carrion-beaked and carrion-clawed themselves!
As Thaddeus spoke, I saw those cardinals,
Archbishops, abbots, royal emissaries,
Ranged in the tainted darkness of their church,
Posturing as the world's high court of justice
And tottering through the motions of a trial
Whose sentence had been writ before its charge.
Guzzlers and sycophants of envious Rome!
Louis of France, for all his saintliness,
Pled for the emperor, and England's voice
Was just though weak. So potent was the suasion
Of Thaddeus when at last they gave him leave
To answer and defend, the council shook,
They say, with conscience-stabbed irresolution. . . .
But Innocent poured out his eloquent hate
And while the organ groaned, the hymns surged up —
As through some fissure cracked in noisy hell —
Those old men dashed their writhing torches down
And in the awful darkness cursed my father. . . .
'Twas here you will recall that Thaddeus stopped,
Sank to his seat and dumbly clutched the table.

And my father's voice leaped out, " Go on, go on!
The sentence? " It was not Thaddeus who answered.
Da Vigna spoke, standing far down the room,
A late arrival here as at the Conclave:
His tones, clear always, never seemed so clear:
" Anathema and Excommunication."
I saw my father smile. Da Vigna saw it.
He paused and spoke again: " And this besides:
The Holy Roman Empire's Emperor,
Frederick, called the Second, is hereby
Deposed — allegiance to him voided, nay,
Forbidden: thus saith the Conclave with one voice."
Lightning — that blinded as it crashed, downward!
There was a deadly daze of silence. It grew.
All gazed toward my father. But he was silent,
And motionless upon the conspicuous throne.
Their stupor turned ferocious restlessness:
Fear that he searched in vain for words to feed them
Smothered my heart and twitched about my nostrils.
But still he did not speak or lift his eyes.
Suddenly swirled the blade-hiss of his voice:
" Arabs, ho there! Fetch here my treasure chests! "
Our wonder was a terror and a stillness
The whole while that they found and brought the chests.
We leaned and saw them by the lowest step
And barely let our eyes seek up to where
He sat and gazed upon them. Then he stood,
And slowly step by step came down — stooping,
Horribly focussed on the treasure chests.
One hand trailed to his girdle's keys and hung,
And he himself unlocked and opened each.

He lifted one by one his sacred crowns,
Jerusalem's, the Kingdom's, last the Empire's,
And held them to the light with fixed filmed eyes,
Then strained about to face us, stealthily.
The spectre of his voice called through a cave:
"They are all here." That hollow sound awoke him:
He straightened, set the great crown on his head,
And mounted to his throne the way he would,
All emperor, of world and self possessed.

How hot then poured his lava eloquence,
Molten and vehement! but back of it
Cold mind, and crafty watching of his hearers.
He probed the vacillant world in probing them —
Those faces brutal, unintelligent,
Ferocious in their avidness to live,
Confused or terrified at Pietro's news.
They listened to his wrath. But at his warning
Of what submission to such arrogance
Boded to them who were themselves enthroned
And could by this same precedent be dashed
From their high stations at an old man's whim —
He set them breathing hard and fingering sword-hilts.
Then it was pitiful, Berard, to see him,
Warmed at their warming, hope to flush their hearts
With the wild rosy splendor of his dream.
He dignified them with the truth — explained
His kingdom of the spirit for the few,
His fancied freedom for the falcon-souled —
As if they could partake of visioning.
They chilled: and slipped vague glances at their neighbors.

And then I caught da Vigna watching them,
The hovering wings of his eyes gray as old ice.
He felt their ebb of ardor, but no sooner
Than Frederick himself, who forthwith changed
And spiced his argument to suit their stomachs.
He challenged Innocent to pull him down,
Dared him to set another in his place,
Swearing he'd hold it as his sacred right
Though old men cursed and quenched their torches out.
Their strength was equal to a torch's quenching,
But not to quenching an imperial sun.
Then on from there of strengths and weaknesses —
The man-power his from Etna to the Rhine,
His fleets, allies, resources, endless treasure
Against the starveling papal regiments,
The flight from Rome, the general disaffection,
The iterated and unanswered calls
For tithes and tribute. Conclaves could convene,
But Victory crowned the strong, and who as strong
In all the armored world as Frederick?
Cheeks flushed and flashing eyes were everywhere:
The hot contagion of his words as always
Had done its work: his last phrase thundering still,
They clashed their swords down on the reeling table,
Tossed up their goblets in a mighty toast,
And shouted, " Death to Rome! Frederick! Frederick! "
He gravely bowed and gravely waved them out
With " Gentlemen, be your sleep calm as mine."

They joined the darkness. With the last one's exit
He sank back in his throne: I kept my place

And waited for his eyes to look for mine.
We were alone: the shadowy hall was empty,
Bleak with disorder, stale with feasting done.
He sat immobile as a carven king:
I feared to rouse him from that fell abstraction
And he seemed not to know I even lived.
The lights waned and the moonlight grew and lengthened
And bars of hollow silver spanned the gloom.
And still we sat apart and no word spoken.
Then I crept down the table to his throne
And stood beneath him, saw his eyes wide open,
But not the eyes I knew. They did not see me.
I mounted one by one the purple steps
And coming to his feet sat there, and leaned
My head against the throne, flush with his knee.
At last I questioned: " What does it mean, my father? "
I thought he had not heard me; then he spoke
From loneliness, across an infinite chasm:
" The end. Darkness ahead. Darkness ahead." —
Words the fewest and most sorrowful
That ever sunk their anchors in my soul!
We were so close! yet I could not reach out
And soothe the grief of his profound despair.
The vultures tear us on our several hills
Which neighbor no two closelier than yields
A perfect view of our most loved one's anguish.
I knew he saw the conclave's condemnation
As the immitigable blow of fate
That crashed down all the fabric of his life
And left his hopes dispowered as a dream.
And I knew what he saw was very truth

Though what I saw was only curling chaos
And nothing clear and nothing of fair promise.
So though the ebbing smoke-drifts of the room
I looked out on the lowlands and the moonlight
And watched the ravelled cloud-banks floating past,
The spindrift of a sunset's storm of color,
And thought of his cloud-splendor now so toppled. . . .
There was much time for many thoughts to stumble
Before he stirred and spoke in that far way,
But now his voice was frayed and slow with pain:
" Save yourself, Enzio. For you there's time.
You are not safe with Helios any more."
My throat swelled suddenly and all my will
Was in the forcing of a voice to answer:
" I will not leave you now; nor ever leave you.
We will fight on as we have fought, together."
His body's quiver was a long time dying:
" We will fight on then, Enzio, my son."
His hand blessed for a moment my bent head.
The torches guttered out; down the long hall,
Across the litter of the banquet table,
The windows poured their caverns of gray fire;
And still he sat, sagged forward, hands on knees,
The imperial crown a red slur round his forehead.
A moon misshapen stumbled down the sky,
Bloody and sick. And there was no more to say. . . .

Another man had broken: not my father.
He fought on, with a difference that grew. . . .
How do we hate iniquity and thrive,
But, hating them that are iniquitous,

Harden and grow ourselves somehow attaint
With the venom hoarded for the unrighteous foe?
Unjust dilemma! We cannot grip an evil
Fleshless, abstract, not cased in him or her
On whom we may lay hands of wrath and ruin!
To not hate wrong rubs out man's one distinction:
Ably to hate it saps the root of reason.
He grew to hate, a clenched, vein-jutting hatred,
And Innocent and them opposed he hated.
The priests will write it in their manuscripts —
For flourish to his catalogue of crimes —
That he was cruel. I have found all men so.
But true it is he hardened after Lyons:
He did not lag in cruelty; indeed,
His old Sicilian temperateness dried up.
The tide was set against him: each new day
Brought new defections, losses, perjured friends,
But still he dominated with his dripping sword
The whole peninsula — and for his camp
Built him a city — " Victory," alas.
That monster citadel he meant as answer,
Insult and challenge to the Conclave's edict.
He could not name its name even to me
Afterwards. Verily, Parma, I could wish
To live, if life of mine could work revenge!
It had not fallen, had I not been elsewhere.
Berard, it is not all the treasure lost,
The scoffing of the world, even the death
Of Thaddeus torn, still living, limb from limb,
That makes so passing pitiful to me
Vittoria's capture. But I am picturing always

His gay return from hunting through the woods.
He was so great a hunter, and its love
Medicined him when most his soul was sickened.
I see him, rested by his weariness,
Riding ahead upon his sweating stallion
With all the rough loud hunters in his wake,
And coming to a clearing on the hillside,
And catching sight below him on the plain
Of acred flames where once Vittoria spread
And running ants that were his armies once.
Humiliation heaped on helplessness!
He never hunted after that, Berard,
And lacked, I know, the sweetening of that
Forgetful wholesomeness. That Parma stole.

Deposed, his honor gone, and Thaddeus slain,
There seemed no residue of misery
That he need blench at. Yet the worst impended.
This incarnator of uncarnate dreams
Had left for fate to pierce only his heart,
And men had thought that was invulnerable.
Men thought so: we knew better. But your eyes
Were spared the sight of it red-riven, smoking —
Would mine had been! They'd have less fear of sleep
Had not his sickness called me to Cremona.
He ailed, and none could find the seat of ailment,
So he exchanged a captive we had got
Of Parma for Pietro's own physician who
Was there, a prisoner — the mutual gift
Made at da Vigna's counsel, nay, his urgence.
I had not seen him since he spoke so clearly.

He'd been too late to speak out at the Conclave,
But heard the sentence, with some horror doubtless.
When his physician came and saw my father
Feeble with fever, twitching on the bedclothes,
Da Vigna was solicitous, but asked
Leave to depart the city that same day
About the empire's business. Leave was granted,
For I was there to act in his behalf.
When he had gone, and with him the physician
To brew a sleeping potion for the night,
An Arab burst into the room, tottered,
Fell at my father's bedside, gripped his shoulder,
And while swift tears of misery smeared his cheeks
Whispered in Arabic some broken message.
My father roused up with a choking cry,
Struck him across the face, and as he fell
Called for the guards to gag him and imprison;
Then fell back on his bed, sweat-cold and shaking.
" Let not da Vigna leave tonight," he gasped.
" Be here with him at dark, and nothing said."
The night came soon, though slowlier than night comes,
And found da Vigna, me, the Arab guards
Assembled in his chamber. It reeked of fever.
But, saying that his health was mended somewhat,
He sat half-dressed, though haggard as I thought,
And calm, except his eyes, blue-bright, unpausing.
Beside him was a table with his papers,
A rush-light, and his ruby-hilted broad-sword.
He was midway in giving us instructions
As to provisioning the eastern army,
When Pietro's good physician padded in,

His hands about a bowl of sleeping draught.
My father smiled: " All sleep is good, but one
Is best. You mean me well? " " Master, with this,"
The leech replied, " you will sleep well till morning."
" Which will break, doubtless, with a trumpet blast,"
My father sneered. " 'Twill take as much to sain me."
Then carelessly to Pietro, " We can trust him? "
Who was as careless in his clear-voiced answer,
" My life is almost hourly in his hands:
I've never found a cause to think him faithless."
My father's snake-arm struck and bit his sword-hilt,
His voice snarled through his nostrils at the leech:
" Then drink it half yourself." The man shrank back,
Sick-green and speechless, horrible with fear.
The drink splashed in his hands, had fallen but
My father clutched it up half-full and called,
" Bring now the prisoner that prays for sleep,"
And instantly from some near room there walked
A blank-eyed prisoner between two Arabs.
My father held the bowl to him and said,
" Drink this, my friend; my hope is you will sleep."
The man said not a word, but drank it down.
" Sirs," my father turned to us, " sit down.
There's patient waiting here for all of us."
So we sat down; the man, too, that had drunk.
Bound in a common cataleptic coil,
Speechless, transfixed, we watched his poor meek face —
Our separate terrors wrestling with our wills
To burst out in a scream and break the nightmare.
At last his eyelids flickered, lowered, closed.
Our senses strained, each one an ear, to catch

The rustle of his breathing. His body slackened,
Wavered and lurched, and toppled to the floor.
He lay there twisted, still, so unreposeful
One longed to make him easy, but none stirred.
And our own spell of hideous quietude
Seemed part of his eternal sprawled discomfort.
The emperor broke it with a voice as dead
As were his eyes and they were tombs: " Pietro,
Lean down and lay your head upon his heart
And tell me if it beats." And Pietro reeled
And sounds clawed in his throat and choked away
And all his body wrinkled back with horror.
But he knelt down and leaned and pressed his ear
Upon the spot where that man's heart had beat.
His eyes grew wide and wider, no more wings
Hovering, then they shut, and when his voice
Rasped through an opening in his throat, it had
No old-time clearness. " It beats no more," he said.
The emperor staggered — thunder might have struck him,
Instead of words just heard. He took one step,
Lunged through the leech's body with his sword,
Who belched up blood, crumpled and fell, stone dead.
The smoking huddle lay across his feet —
He spurned it off and spoke: " Take out the dung."
Then tottered, stayed him on his bleeding sword,
And closed his eyes, and held his hand upon them,
As if gone blind of infinite despair,
But opened them and plunged them into Pietro's
And held them there, as though for all his grief
There must be comfort in those once friendly depths.
But Pietro flung himself face down and clasped

His feet and cried, " Pardon, Imperial Master,
Pardon! " The sword dropped from my father's hand
And both his hands groped upward to his throat
And worried there and tore his collar back:
His eyes closed in their hollows, his features worked.
He strangled so before he could groan out:
" Another word — not that — another word! "
And then his reason reeled and stumbled back,
Calling one word as if there were no other:
" Confessed, confessed, confessed, confessed — O God! "
Da Vigna crushed his face against his arm,
Shuddered, then lay quite still, so did not see
The emperor stoop above him, gaze, recoil,
And draw his foot back with a snarl of loathing.
Berard, Berard, I would forget his change
From agony to rage and hate, though just!
He said no more than it was true to say,
Pouring the words like acid over Pietro,
Words you can guess, deserved — oh, well deserved —
And yet, when heard, unworthy of my father.
Let me not think of that! O God! O God!
I shrank from him, he did not seem my father,
But some gross beast that had gone beastly mad —
His flaccid mouth too weak to hold its water,
And all his face a pouch of flesh that glistened!
And, oh, the beastly cry that ended it:
" Burn out his eyes and bind him to a mule
And drive him, socket-empty, through the world —
An epigram of Frederick's love turned hate! " . . .
Justice, indeed, but who is ripe for justice?
Pietro had fainted when the Arabs touched him

The emperor watched him heaved out like a corpse,
Then blindly motioned us to leave the room —
And I left gladly, left him palsied, shrunken;
So even I was dimmed with treachery
And let my spirit falter in its love.

My bed was in a chamber close to his,
A bed that night no sleep had tucked and pillowed.
I lay and killed the horror in my soul,
And reckoned up his measureless misery.
I saw what I had never seen before,
That he was young no longer. He had looked
Almost an old man when they lifted Pietro —
Slack and uncertain, creased and gray with strain.
I had not thought he'd ever not be hale
Or wear the taint of time in any crevice.
Not death, but mind and body's stealthy crumble
Before they slough and fall is nature's worst.
And nothing twitches so the heart as seeing
In one we love the wall's first visible crack.
I wept for him, Berard, and as I wept
His great voice suddenly burst across the stillness
And he was calling, " Enzio, Enzio, Enzio! "
As hell's poor damned must call on their first night.
I rushed into his chamber. He was sitting
Upon the bedside, clutching it for prop,
His mighty shoulders stooping, and his head
Bowed on his breast. I ran to him, dropped down,
And saw his eyes — my father's eyes, Berard! —
Smoking with terror! He seized my hands, my arms,
Felt up my face, across my hair — oh, blindly —

Whispering " Is it you, Enzio? Is it you? "
I slipped my arm around him, steadied him.
But still he shook, and whispered huskily:
" He knew me. My heart lay beating in his hand.
He was the faithful Peter of our Kingdom.
He did not hate me: could he love, he loved me;
But he was overborne by the turned tide.
There was no anchor to his intellect:
Truth he saw, but could not hook its grapples
Under his heart. The long time that I prospered,
Their outcry moved him not: but at the end
The universal condemnation shook him,
And when the filthy world cried out ' Unclean '
He could not feel me clean, although he knew it,
So slackened in his faith, doubting, doubting,
And at my ebb of fortune did — what he did!
If Pietro can desert me, who will stay?
If he can be untrue, where look for faith?
There're daggers in each doorway, in each aisle
Spears, and each window has drawn arrows. Oh,
No cup but reeks with poison and no heart
But rears with viper hate and treachery!
No way to turn — no going back or forward —
And none to wade the blood and darkness with me!
Enzio, Enzio, we are alone, and you —
Will you be going too? Will you? Will you?
The way I walk leads to a ghastly nowhere,
But, oh, beseech you, leave me not alone!
Be pitiful, for all the love I bear you —
My son, my son! "
Berard, the noblest of all emperors

Lay sobbing in my arms like some poor child,
And I was healing him of dreadful tears
With words my own would hardly let me utter —
Mere words, though weak in wisdom, strong in love.
No night of mine can ever be as choked
With misery and helplessness again.

So wounded mortally, he still could live
Because I clove to him. Then I was taken. . . .
All that his son could do I did in that
Last battle: more than any but his son
Could dream of doing. The Modanese betrayed us.
There was no help. Their dead lay tiered around me
And ours had left me friendless by the evening.
I could not tell my blood from blood I'd emptied
And I had fainted when they captured me.
There was no help. Fate meant to break him so
With the one cruelty unused, but hoarded.
I knew he threatened and implored, and vainly,
For I was brag and safeguard of Bologna:
Assaulted, she would tear me limb from limb
Before his maddened eyes, and there's not gold
Sufficient in the earth to ransom me.
And, after that, I knew he could not stay
And fight the fight out in the north alone,
But would drag back like some great wounded beast
Into the Kingdom's lair and sanctuary. . . .
Yet, all his heart was homesick for had gone,
Vanished in cloud-dust, dust of death, or prison:
His kingdom was a boundary, bounding nothing.
He died because he had no heart to live:

Life was unworthy of his presence in it. . . .
I'm glad he died away from the loud world,
With twilight woods around him, in your arms;
And glad his mind was steady to the end
And he knew Death. . . . It was a kingly meeting —
Death and my father. . . . You say he had his bed
Borne to that window of the hunting lodge
That faces west, and lay there open-eyed,
In some great revery beyond your ken,
Watching the wintry sunset winnow out
From red to gray behind the keen still trees;
And then his eyes called to you and you stooped,
And heard his words, but two: "Tell Enzio."
He closed his lids, regretless that no strength
Would open them again. . . . When he walked through
The portals of Death's purple-raftered house,
I know the other guests arose and stood. . . .

My words have bridged the two walls of the night.
The far one crumbles now. . . . Come, look, Berard.
Aldebaran has gone with his companions.
An old moon, blue with cold, limps up the east,
Thin as the new. He will be overtaken,
And halfway up his mountain die, in the sun . . .
A beggar's death . . . an old man's death, alone. . . .
Old age which should be but a hill's descent,
May be an ever-upward mountain toil,
By night, through empty cold, in loneliness. . . .
By count, Berard, my years are thirty: but
My living days ahead are all old age.
Here is a crass unthoughtedness, a waste,

A mere continuing that is not life,
Miserable to me, to no man helpful. . . .
Our utmost is a stave of noble song
Scrawled blindly on the scrap of page allowed
And tossed into the sea — unlearned, unpraised,
Of no avail. Yet it could be ignoble:
I'll not have mine default in fortitude
By ending it. I'll let the stave be rounded,
As if my father were my listener. . . .

I cannot see by what integrity
High Heaven annihilated so his efforts!
Unless there be no heaven — and that I'll grant
Sooner than that his vision's fate was just! . . .
A vision's own validity and worth
Has no transmuting power to turn it facts;
And, even turned, with all the needed aid
Of accident combined with dominant will,
Its best escapes: its second best may live
And for a dubious cycle shed its lustre.
But his was buttressed by all things save chance,
And there's no tatter left, no single gleam.
What hope for this wrong world if such things be?
What are so hemmed by horror, pressed by darkness,
That there's no lighted calm where we may pause
And see our evil destinies in bulk —
Bathed in an awful loveliness, perhaps,
And part of some transcending glimpsed coherence.
There is no certain thing I can lay hold on
And say, " This, this is good! This will I worship! "
Except my father. For he intended like

A god: or, since I see no signs of gods,
If some day earth shall house divinities
In guise of men, or in some guise I guess not,
They shall be minded, willed, and souled like him.
And so despite life's infamy and failure
I thank whatever may be thanked that I
Was heaved up from the insentient void and saw
In him divinity, though marred and baffled.
It seems now nothing else in life was worth
The seeing. What the crop is of his sowing
I am not seer enough to speculate:
I only know the grain was golden and
The earth is culpable if there's no harvest. . . .
Darkness; darkness; and for me no hope
Of any light, unless there be some place
For tarrying, where he will tarry for me.

Now let me kneel, old man, and clasp your knees
And bend my head the way I learned when little,
And you will bless me through your falling tears. . . .
Ah, you and I are all that now remain
Of his heart's Kingdom, so we must keep worthy. . . .
Go now, Berard. The waiting's empty, but
The end is sure, and we have much to dream on.

EPILOGUE

This wind upon my mouth, these stars I see,
The breathing of the night above the trees,
Not these nor anything my senses touch
Are real to me or worth the boon of breath.
But all the never-heard, the never-seen,
The just-beyond my hands can never reach,
These have a substance that is stout and sure,
These brace the unsubstantial sliding world,
And lend the evanescent actual
An air of life, a tint of worth and meaning.
Shall dust, fortuitously blown into
A curve of moon or leaf or throat or petal
And seeding back to vacancy and dust,
Content my soul with its illiterate
And lapsing loveliness? Or tired knowledge
Make credible the hard decree of living?
Oh, I have heard a golden trumpet blowing
Under the night. Another warmth than blood
Has coursed, though briefly, through my intricate veins.
Some sky is in my breast where swings a hawk
Intemperate for immortalities
And unpersuaded by the show of death.
I am content with that I cannot prove.

PART IV

NEW POEMS

CONFIDANTS

Rejoice, my heart, that the stars do not comprehend you,
That they march on their mighty courses, serene and terrible,
Unvexed by your sorrow, untarnished by your desires.
You may spread your pain like a purple cloth before them
And their silver and golden feet will brush it lightly
As they brush the cloths of the grass which is more beautiful.
You may cry aloud to them your dolor and desolation,
And though your cry were intolerable and keen as Israfel's,
They will not heed it, high-hearted in the roar of ebbing chaos.
Even your self-pity, shining like a gift and shameless,
You may bring them without evil, for they, they only of your comrades,
Resist the infection of sorrow, the contagion of tears.

RECOGNITION

Quietly, silently passing, at twilight, when streets are crowded,
Ah, the faces I see, the sad beautiful faces of men,
With the haze of their dream or their love or their sorrow tenderly on
    them,
With the charmed wistful shadows and hollows on cheek and temple,
Strangers to me, passing from dark into dark, unreturning!
Would I could lay on their twilight lids the kiss of peace,
But they pass, and I can only call after them " Brother, brother."

THREE APRIL NOCTURNES

1. THE BREEZE

This night of air like warm finger-tips touching
Sleepily my cheek or asleep in my shoulder's hollow,
I remember the kisses they gave me in tenderness or passion,
Never in love, the ones they could spare me, forgetful,
And I am thankful for each, regretting nothing,
Only wishing they lay on my mouth again
To-night when the moist buds are uncrinkling in starlight
And the air is touching my cheek like finger-tips warm and
   sleepy.

2. THE MOCKING-BIRDS

All night they wake and sing on the cold branches,
Sometimes a mere cadenza of delight, a phrase,
Or hours long of glittering bravado.
The silver-breasted stars in their long swarming,
Endlessly migratory, lighting never
Spring after spring, float over them unheeding;
Under the eaves, in the cautious green of the myrtle
No lover-bird rouses from sleep to listen:
All but the singers sleep, and the dark is deaf.
Nights when the jonquils bloom and the April iris
They wake and sing their cold rash ecstasy
To their own hearts, girded with terrors and lonely —
And I in the spring night listening blush for a coward.

3. THE RAIN

The rain has come and gone, and the night is breathing:
There is humble joy in the little things that grow,
The slow trees meditate and burgeon,
Far off the tiny frogs are happy in chorus,
The last rain-drops tap like fairy hammers,
Slowly the air sweetens with stealthy perfume.
So it will always be when the night is April:
Sorrow is never strong and tears are ended;
Only the heart is untranquil, that soon will sleep.

STIRRUP CUP

I whisper to my heart words of courage
And it hears and arises and fares on again —
Not like a soldier striding to battle,
But like a pilgrim old and weary.
I say to my heart very softly and tenderly:
" Truly the shrine that we sought is a sepulchre,
But holy, perhaps, as we have been told.
It is ignoble that we, you and I,
Should sit in the dust of the roadside and weep.
We have seen stars and sunsets,
We have heard birds and thunder,
Many have been the travellers,
We have had noble companions.
Perhaps again (but the end is soon)
We will see, and hear, and hold lofty converse.
But even alone, in darkness and silence,
Remember we haughtily draw
The ice-silver of pride from far sources:
We come not of weaklings and weepers.
And there is no weakness to conquer
Till strength is taken away.
We are strengthless, unweaponed, but we will go on."

AT SEA

Endure, my heart, endure: that is the ultimate courage.
So much is taken, and the rest seems better gone;
And in the hurly of the dissolute and dreadful world
Little remains of fair and wise, of just and simple.
Break but the shackles and the quailing sound is heard
Of anchor chains that break. The harbors of the past,
Silted, have grown too shallow for our deepening keels,
Or we have lost the star that guided to their entrance.
Nothing is compass to our destinies, unless
The very fortitude of that cursed mariner
Who knows no port but death, yet fights the sail and sweats
And holds the rudder true, be of itself a chart
To guide at last his haggard bark, amazedly,
Beneath the samite wall of some moon-vestured town
Where towers stand, more tranquil than somnambulists.
Be brother to the mighty mariners, my heart:
So stoutly sail that there should be a silver port.

HILL–TOP BY THE SEA

Sickened and soiled, with all the lustre gone,
I have come back to the hill-top by the sea
And find it beautiful still, and so I know
Not all of me is dead. This too I know:
For me the god is here, in loneliness,
With an empty sea below, ribboned with wind,
And a sunlight, grave and pure, in the olive trees —
Here, and not down in the smoking jungles of men.
Let me remain, O doomed brief body of mine,
Itching for love, faithless to me you hold,
Crying out to cup the dark head of a lover
In the curve of your arm. It is late, late, and the light
Has gone from your throat, the honey-scent from your hair.
Let us remain till the long night finds us here.
A moon will come, parting the olive branches,
And lay on your breast, in the curve of your quiet arm,
A wreath of light, tender as no dark head.
But I, while yet your lids with my tears are shining,
I will steal down without you, among the shadows,
And come to the sea and pause. May the god be waiting.

FOURTEEN SONNETS

Not to be naming you in all my prayers
Has made me prayerless, pagan, atheist;
Not to be knowing I am of your cares
Has loosed a ghost with eyes of amethyst
Into the regal day. The only thread,
Now broke, that bounden me to life was you,
So I am free now to consort with dead
Invisible lovers in their hushed purlieu.
O I am free now to regard the rise
From ocean of the round and rosy moon,
Muse on her narrow length of dragon dyes
Like Clytemnestra's carpet — Take the boon!
I saw as much last night, with you away:
The moon was only round, the ocean gray.

Here life pays peace and ecstasy for tithe:
The dissonant trumpets of the world are mute
And God is but an old man with a scythe
And love the faltering fancy of a flute.
To lie with kissing lashes and confuse
The silver olives and the golden sun,
To sort the greens and purples from the blues
When the lean racers of the south wind run,
Rounding abreast the bulging Apennine,
And burst upon the clapping bay — ah, these
Are all the drudgeries of this demesne
Whose boundary is music and the sea's.
Ye starved and hurt, ye hives of busy ghosts,
Would I could lend your ills this sea, these coasts.

Where through the olive trees I see bright shawls
And bathers laughing in the beryl bay,
Lovers more bold for tilted parasols
And waters summery and cerulean, lay
The hoarse and sweating legionnaires of Rome
Breaking their march. When they had marched their last,
Algerian pirates made of this their home
And heckled Genoa from here, and passed.
In some pale after-day of Arctic fear
When all the glittering tribes of us have thinned,
One of our last, perhaps, will wander here
Beneath the sockets of the stars and wind,
And facing seawards in the thickening night
Pray the old prayer to the last god " More light! "

Portofino.

Beloved and alien, gaze with me on the sea:
It kneels before the moon whose crimson blade
Rests on its million shoulders. But for me
The image of that lunar accolade
Is not the one your eyes bring in to you:
It varies by the flinching of a wave,
A widening iris, or a lens more true —
Or, if identical, the fact how prove?
If thus the tangible we may not share,
How hope the gorgeous fabrics of the soul
To spread before each other, or how dare
Another's undecipherable scroll
To con? Even in love we must confess
No understanding and great loneliness.

What disputations doth my spirit hold,
Contending with itself of this and that,
Laggard, alas, in action, but most bold
To storm celestial citadels with chat!
Now will it hale the villain flesh to bar,
Condemning it for all its own transgressions,
Holding itself a virgin winter-star,
Eclipsed but by poor body's vile obsessions.
Now when much weariness hath done it spite
It calleth body as the only leech,
Beggeth of him a music, or a sight
Curative — leaves in rain or thundering beach —
And ever in its loneliness it cries,
" Show me her hands, her mouth, her pitiful eyes."

When I allow my schoolèd eyes to lift
And see the beautiful ones of earth drift past
With parted lips and scooped wings of the swift
Along their temples — each lovelier than the last —
Seeing the wistful hunger in their eyes,
I love those damnèd ladies sweet of heart
Who draw the rippling curtains at sunrise
And watch the stranger, solaced by their art,
Sleeping and warm and childish: I would teach
Their kindness to my heart and solace too,
Like Magdala and Cressid, all and each,
To each unfaithful, but to all most true.
But there are some whose fortune is to be
Lonely: no beautiful one has need of me.

Let me confess I am no Launcelot —
But not to you confess, or you, or you,
The many I have loved, for you have got
What share of me you asked, your every due,
And we are quits. But to my secret soul
I make confession — and absolve as well —
That little parts and never the great rôle
I've played, and often, in love's carnival.
Well cast, no doubt. But I have read, somewhere,
A long time since, and liked, a sadder plot
Of two that wept or kissed on a dark stair
Hearing the winds howl over Camelot. . . .
Thou Maker of hearts flawed and dissonant,
The pain left out of mine — this I resent.

Knowing you give yourself without desire —
No golden turmoil and no fevered shame —
I take you with a four-fold kindled fire,
My salty torment coloring the flame.
Your acquiescence I reward with all
The secret riches only love should see,
Share beauty with you, run before you call,
Make your desires my one idolatry.
O I have made myself so rare a lover
That though I get from you nor praise nor blame
The world applauds, and, seeing but the cover,
Gives to the bawdy thing a sacred name.
But not for you I play this zealous rôle:
From cold-fanged lust somehow it saves the soul.

Though we be breasted shallowly, to hold
Deciduous loves that live their sweetness out,
Impotent by dimension to enfold
One mighty love and single, never doubt
But there are breasts can chalice love's full tide
With all its weight of wind and stars and rain,
Though lodgment for a surge so deep, so wide
Demands the hollow where some sea has lain.
We are but woodland pools whose shallow urns
One summer empties and one April fills,
Doubling a neighborhood of flowers and ferns,
Devout for any star the great dark spills.
We are for wayfarers to drink from and forget,
Parting again the branches low and wet.

All that is lovely is incredible,
No sooner seen or heard or touched than gone
And not believed in by the mind too full
Of mirrors to recall what has withdrawn.
I am so filled with ghosts of loveliness
That I could furbish out and populate
A vacant star, so that the gods would press
To gaze and memorize and duplicate.
But here, alone, with fog about my heart,
Of all the beauty I have seen so plain
I seek to summon up so small a part
Two hands could hold it, and I seek in vain.
I only know your eyes and mouth and hair
Are beauty's own: I cannot see them, dear.

With what unyielding fortitude of heart
We tap the prison walls to find escape,
Measure the thickness, calculate and chart, —
As if mole eyes could read the meagre tape!
Long after our unteemèd brain's forgot
The hope of star or sun or crystal air,
We fumble at the hinges of the plot
And cipher on the whence and how and where.
Our knowledge foots no sum: our seasoned pen
Writes question-marks we dry with our last breath.
Lavish in horror to the race of men,
Thou makest a boon, O God, of horrible death, —
Yet canst not wring this cry from minds mature
"Let us seek anodynes, for there's no cure."

Not the blue flagstones of eternal space,
Sprinkled a little way with frugal fire,
Confound my mind, for there's no mind can pace
Our visible moiety of space entire
From earth to moon, from moon to Formilhaut
And out and out beyond the phosphorent weave
Of nebulæ and the last golden tow
Of suns pulsing at anchor, that can conceive
Ending or no beyond. A hope is here,
Ambiguous, obscure, but still a hope:
If mind's machinery, this thinking gear
Boasts the eternal for its mould and scope,
Is he eternal that I thought could die —
This flash of dew, this frosty breath, this I?

I have no patience, no philosophy
To heal at all the wound that we call life:
One after one the anodynes for me
Have failed. Still as of old I see the strife,
Savage and sad, but have forgot its cause
Nor glimpse its outcome any more. The stare
Of truth has not revealed immutable laws
Or far beneficences or the care
Of any intellect, alert, serene.
Instead, these I am sure of as I wait:
Pain, the hot-sanded heart's one evergreen;
Ignorance, rubbing slick the cell of fate.

On, in the dark, then; cloak the decent scars:
The cage of darkness shows, not hides the stars.

Chart back as best he might the way he'd come
And not a turn but still seemed best to choose,
Yet he had reached a wilderness, wherefrom
He must escape or all the struggle lose.
The urgency to act was thick upon him,
But still he paused to place the past mistake:
Inevitable blameless by-gones stun him,
His loyalties to shaping justice break.
At last he saw and took, like one quite tired,
The path ahead, obscure and full of stress:
To see was easy, but to take required
The solemn fortitude of hopelessness.

His clothes are shiny now that once were napped:
The liveliest beast grows somewhat seedy, trapped.

PROMETHEAN

All day the vultures sit and tear my heart
Among the scorched unearthly tremulous peaks:
All night it heals and grows with mystic art
Pasture again for purple hammering beaks.

How long will days return with latticed light
And brassy plumes upon my side like fleece?
However long, longer still the night,
The healing longer, and the long dark peace.

TREES

I'll push the iron heavens back,
I'll lift them from my shoulders' rack,
And walk awhile and be at ease
And fellow with the sober trees.
They wear the morning's sequined wet
As calmly as the turbulent jet
When lavender and silver eels
Leap from the drunken tempest's creels.
Each battles only for the space
Demanded by his destined grace
And when that width of sky is got
Envies no other tree his lot.
No sound he makes not musical,
No thing he has not beautiful;
When comes what comes to each, alone,
He stands and dies, and makes no moan . . .
For me by useless riddles stung,
Unwise in silence and in tongue,
Beating at walls I think are doors,
Neglecting mine for heaven's chores,
Wisdom and patience might be found
In trees content to stand their ground.

CERTAIN CASUALS

Breastful of shadow,
How proudly they go,
Secret in sorrow,
Silent in woe,

Never a light
Along lids to denote
All of the tears
Caught back in the throat.

Regal the place is —
Heaven or hell —
Fit to receive them,
Wounded so well.

SONG

Bring them no song from Faerie,
Lend them no dreamy lies —
These have a dread in their bosoms,
These have a hurt in their eyes.
No scarlet skeins nor patterns,
No scents nor sounds nor dyes —
Tears make warm the bosom,
Kisses heal the eyes.

TO A DOGWOOD IN SUMMER

    They tell me that essential you
        Is just essential me —
    Electrons shifting, you'd be man
        And I a twinkling tree.

    That could have happened easily
        Odd twenty years ago,
    But you, to match me, must have worn
        Your moonlight and your snow.

CHIMES

Her shadows are rimmed with silver,
And there is wild beautiful sunlight in her anger;
Her injustice is some virtue in excess,
And the dapple of dew is on her passion.
Because of her I am like the morning for laughter
And like the morning-glory vine for innocence;
Rain-washed leaves might fillet my forehead
And a dream could hover there.
Always I seem to be lying
On the green soft meadow of the world
Beneath the blue bell of heaven where the birds hurry,
Repeating lauds and magnificats and glorias:
The blue bell of heaven is pealing,
The blue bells of the morning-glory ring out hosannas,
It is Easter morning
And my heart is a steeple with chimes.

A LITTLE HYMN

All in the blue, blue morning
    Our Lady led our Lord
Whose eyes were blue like flowers
    Along a lilied sward.
He touched the lily throats and laughed
    Like any blond wee child;
    Like any mother, she
    Touched his and smiled. . . .
    I have a morning-glory,
    I have a golden gourd —
    I need our Lady
    And a blond wee lord.

        L. P.

"How many trees in your forest?"
    "One:
    The rest are saplings
    That preen in the sun."
"What happens in your forest
    When storms run?"
    "Odd,
    The saplings add hardly
    A leaf to the sod,
But the tree bows like Jacob
    Wrestling with God."

ALTITUDE

A star, a cloud, a bird, a bell
Know that the world does very well,
But snakes and flitter-mice and men
Perceive it as a noisome pen.
Sky and steeple and top o' tree
Are places where I long to dwell
    And do, infrequently,
But house of earth and field and fen,
Fair for night-stops now and then,
    Are usual home to me.
No wonder but by fit and spell
I think the world does very well.

PAN REJECTED

There will be other kisses on your eyes
    But none like mine,
And every kiss will be a shadow kiss
    Because of mine.
Your larkspur eyes with tears another brings
    Will surely shine,
But they refused my purple shrouds of sorrow,
    A gift divine.
Mortal you are, who might have been, a moment,
    Mine.

RECOMPENSE

Beaten, wounded, like to die,
Last of the lost battalion, I
Pour salt into my quaking wound,
Like my horn, red-gleaming, mooned,
And breathe a blast my brethren hear
Beyond these tumbled hills of fear.

In that far naked purple land
They lift to lip a musing hand:
" Defeat " they say, " defeat again,
The ancient doom, the ancient pain,"
— But louder than the victor's jibe —
" The ancient courage of the tribe."

DIRGE

Tuck the earth, fold the sod,
Drop the hollow-sounding clod.
Quiet's come; time for sleeping,
Tired out of mirth and weeping,
Calmed at last of mirth and weeping.
Tuck the earth, fold the sod;
Quiet's here, maybe God.

SHROUD SONG

Only asters gone to seed,
Goldenrod and fennel-weed,
Make her meagre diadem,
Brede her snowy cuffs and hem.
Stitch the blossoms gone to feather
On her breast where frost's the weather,
Here a sprig and there a spray —
Loveliness has gone its way.
There are those who had as lief
Be buried with remembered grief
As live a long long time with it
Stuck in the live heart it has split.
Asters here. — Her only care
Was breathing anything but air;
Her only wish — let's lay them slanted,
So — a simple one, and granted.

THRENODY

All has been said that need be said, all has been done.
Let us return through the fields she loved in the sorrowless sun,
And steady our hearts if we may, our hearts so many, yet one.

Not for forgetting she'd ask, to spare us our brief pain:
She knew the Lethe in all sorrow; she knew the gain,
The flower that blows but by the flower-forgotten rain.

Because of her, life was sweeter: that be the whole of our praise —
Tenderness wrought in a few, a few but for all of their days.
Than that is it fairer at last to have honors, anthems, and bays?

Let us touch hands and part. If simple words can bless
May ours through the mothering grass fall softly and caress:
Earth, lie gently on a heart all gentleness.

FOR RIP WHO DIED MAD

When I go down to Acheron,
    A tired lonely shade,
I'll wish the hand of some sweet ghost,
    Once dear, in mine were laid;

And ferrying that murky flood
    The valiant scorn to drink,
I'll strain to see the dead I love
    Down at the landing's brink.

Far off in blue and silver glens
    Where melts the folded mist,
They will be loitering blissfully
    In cloaks of amethyst.

But as my prow scrapes on the marl,
    One watcher faithful, quaint,
Will dash to meet me who am still
    His master, friend, and saint.

And Rip with paws upon my breast
    And warm breath on my hair
Will tell with little snuggled whines
    How long was waiting there,

And how the madness is quite gone
    That turned his heart untrue.
I shall have lost, please Proserpine,
    Somewhat of madness, too.

ON A THEME FROM SAPPHO

Evening brings all things home that bright day scattered —
The lamb, the kid, the child, each to its mother.
You, you only, evening brings not home,
But comes, for me, without the evening star.

AT DELPHI

This same white snake of road the great dead trod,
Each with some dolorous burden such as mine:
Each prayed of Helios, the healing god,
A cure, an answer, some one heartening sign.

Here Agamemnon stood and Œdipus,
Here I, and Nicias, and Pericles.
The selfsame answer came to each of us:
I learn as little now, as then did these.

Yet they that sought for comfort, and in vain,
Returned, and lived, and mostly found life good,
But, good or ill, labored and took their pain
As if their acre were the Sacred Wood.

And it is well to know that there's no grief
A god may pluck away and heal us from
And none too great to bear, for all are brief,
And we are kingliest when most they come.

THREE OLD TUNES

1

I have no knowledge what it was
    That Atlas stood upon,
The time he hove the burly world
    And held it in the sun —
Ignorance that alone prevents
    My shouldering as much,
Who reel to lift sunflower-high
    A bubble-soul or such.

2

Damocles, friend Damocles,
Felicitous in single doom,
High in the dark of my own room
So many sword-blades tug and tease
I envy luck like Damocles'.

3

I knew Midas, I knew him well,
I am familiar with his hell:
A secret cankered in his heart,
By speech he thought to ease the smart
And chose for hearers of his shame
Reeds that suck mud and have no name,
Fancying though they'd shed no tear

They might than man (his brother dear)
Calumniate less tauntingly
God's curse and his deformity.
(Midas, Midas, couldn't you guess?
Cracked bells should be clapperless.)

MEDUSA

There is a tale of brow and clotted hair
Thrust in the window of a banquet room
Which froze eternally the revellers there,
The lights full on them in their postured doom:
The queen still held the carmine to her lips,
The king's mouth stood wide open for its laugh,
The jester's rigid leer launched silent quips;
Only a blind man moved and tapped his staff.
I cannot guess that physiognomy
The sight of which could curdle into stone
The gazer, though pities, horrors, terrors I
Have made encounter of and sometimes known.
But I knew one who turned to stone with terror
Of facing quietly a flawless mirror.

CRETAN IDYL

See the grasshoppers, flame-colored, beautiful,
Singing and flying in the harsh sunlight,
On the heights of Phæstos, Phæstos trembling with sun.
Hear the click of their wings, flame-colored,
And watch them swarming and singing
Where once the high-built palace towered and sang,
Where now the rubble whitens in glare.
The dark blue sea is yonder
With mints and thyme and grasses,
And yonder down in the valley
The plane trees pool their shadow,
The olives sprinkle a shifting lace,
And the cypresses like silence
Lay a finger of shade.
Surely if I had wings,
I should go slithering down
Where the rose-laurels wade in the pasture,
Their perfume hazy about them,
Heavy with bloom and drowsy,
Too beautiful, ah, to think of.
Why are they crowding here,
Shutting, unshutting their wings,
Here on the shadowless cliff-top
Where only the thistle is thriving,
Blue through all of its body,
Hot blue like a twist of the sky?
The thistles, the parched pale grasses,

These and the dead acanthus,
These are all that remain
Of the garlands and wreaths of Phæstos,
On the shattered tomb of Phæstos.
Why are they here with their singing
And not on the steep of Ida
Where chalk-marks of snow attest
The infinite ravage of summer?
Ah, these are the people of Minos,
The beautiful flame-colored Cretans of old,
Who sang through the palace and danced in the
    dædal days,
In the delicate days before Troy.
And now they cry through the palace,
Drunk with the harsh desolation,
Mad with the terrible sunlight,
Calling for Minos the king,
Calling for sweet Ariadne,
In the empty desolate sunlight,
Flashing their flame-colored wings.

ON AN ANTIQUE LITTORAL

Beauty gone, and beauty gone,
    And gallant wisdom lost —
Crowns the race so hardly won,
    Twines of phantom frost!

Sappho and Empedocles,
    Time's kleptomaniac clan
Coffers their gold where golden sleep
    Knossos and Yucatan.

Dreams that found their way in stone,
    Cool mesmerists of peace,
Or flushed to plumage in a song,
    Or crimsoned Parian Greece,

Loveliness dissuaded from
    The locked and stubborn air —
What rifling of the golden urn,
    Our ransom from despair!

Learn again, and lose again,
    Create, and then destroy —
For knowledge is the race's game
    And loveliness its toy.

A LEGEND OF LACEDÆMON

He stood with the screen of trees betwixt him and the summit,
The oak-trees of his father, old as time and bronze,
But vehement silver now where the moonlight sprinkled the
        leaves with silver
And even the ebon snakes of the trunks and branches
Had markings of silver and burned where they curved.
Beyond the screen, where his somber gaze thrust vainly,
Eternal dark and hush, the place of the god,
Dread abode of his father, under the stars.
He spoke, and the untrembling silver of the trees
Shivered: " My brother is dead." The silence healed,
Like lake-water where a sword thrusts and withdraws.
He waited. Again his low words shook and died away:
" I am your son, and you have slain my brother."
The tangle of the trees plunged in a panic breathing
And reared, the rapid silver of their undersides quaking like mail;
But the words clove them large and quiet, for the god spoke:
    " The beautiful children of the earth perish:
    It is the law. And brief is sorrow."
But the elder and immortal of the Dioscuri
Lowered not his head, and the long pallor of his throat
Shone like marble, only the hollow at its base in shadow:
" My sorrow has no mortal element to briefen it.
Send into hell, not unpitiful god, and fetch my brother back."
An ocean sigh from the core of dark took tone: " To die again? "
As a young hunter lost in the woods, in the twilight forest,
Passing the craggy mouth of some gray cave,

Feels the cold river of ghosts flow out and eddy about him
And draws back shuddering, his sidelong eyes gone gray —
So Pollux shrank, and cold flooded him.
But anger followed, and thrust him one pace nearer,
So the shadow of a leaf lay in his outstretched palm;
"Then, one by one, you will strike down my heart's belovèds —
They mortal, I deformed by immortality — until
Parting's repeated anguish wean me of love!
Bring not my brother back, O god, if he must die again
And I must watch a second horror film his eyes
And touch his eyelids down and know they will not lift,
But take instead my immortality;
Deliver me to hell and him release to earth.
You slew him when he seemed to me
For all his manhood but a little boy
Who'd just made treasure of the wild bee's comb
And dipped his finger in its honey, once.
Let him live out the natural little span
Of his own kind, the warm high-hearted life of earth,
Even to the cruel ebb and break of age;
And I will take his place and sit in weary hell,
Nor plead for change, immortal god."
Vainly he waited answer —
The dark behind the steepled silver of the oak-trees
Tolled with silence. His anger ebbed.
Down the gigantic undulations of Olympos
The moonlight streamed in quietness, and far, far down
Seeped through the patterned woods
And pooled about the timid outlander's unlighted hut
And brimming through the sedgy pastures far below
Piled with gray glister of innumerable sheaves

The mead of the infertile sea.
Through the long levels of the air
The earth-sounds rose, infrequent and unearthly:
The loud cicada of the goatherd's shout,
The thud where ocean in her sleep
Flings one arm up the shore,
The warning from mid-air the leader of the wild-geese sounds
Piloting through the smoke of smouldering Troy
His solemn echelons.

Pollux heard the signal of the bird
As he stood at the portal of the unmerciful god,
And pain bowed his beautiful head and closed his eyes:
For he remembered how in Lacedæmon
When the first film of ice clinked on the marshes
And grass was stiff and morning blue with cold,
He lay in the saw-grass with his laughing brother
As the honking flights drew in;
Together whispering they lay and peered and counciled
Till the seething wings stormed in and thundered above their
    covert,
When crying aloud they leaped, and loosened the long clean
    arrows.
He remembered, and bowed, alone in the moonlight;
His heart was founded within him, the fresh wound bled,
And he turned to the god again, for otherwhere
There was no turning and no hope at all.
His voice plead through his words:
" You will not bring him back . . . Then let me go
And be with him in hell, for hell with him
Is sweeter than the earth without."

The words broke there; his sorrow's reason went unsaid;
But they had been in Lacedæmon, their dear home,
Twin sprays of apple-bloom
When rain has wetted them and they seem younger still.

Hopelessly he stood now nor deemed the god would speak
The revocation of his doom or let him search
The draughty twilight land of Dis for Castor, lost.
So when no sound breathed from the black recess
But the shadows blotched immovably the sand
And the leaf-light shone unsplinteringly,
He turned and with slow hesitant footsteps made toward the
          slope,
The deep and chasm of the pearl-gray air before him.
But where the crest declines, he paused, wheeled,
His rapid steps returning spattered the sand to silver.
Into the shadow of the branches, into the sacred shadow, he
          plunged
And the leaves, affrighted, dappled his loveliness.
Leaning, he clung to the midmost branch, and his words
          poured urgently:
"Ah, piteous god, vexed with dooms and lonely,
Hear me, and read my pain's petitioning
Not in my words, but in the script where it is written, here!
Hateful to me is hell, and the drear nightmare of the dead,
My veins teem with the rank cold ichor of the gods
Which heals with heartlessness
And lets them bear with laughter
The eternal misery outspread.
In the sweet ways of earth, in the long years,
I would forget my brother, or remember

With tenderness unvenomed of all pain.
I would live on in leafy Lacedæmon
With new companions and the olden zest,
Renewed, eternal, lordly in strength,
And tinder to the spark of hot adventure.
Felicities ahead, on the dancing floor of the cymballed sun,
Even with Castor gone, allure me more
Than faint companionship with him among the shades.
This is the truth, the shameful truth of wisdom
That rowels to rebellion all my heart.
But god, my father, O lonely god,
He is the lonesomest of all your ghosts!
Life to him was my companionship,
And now, bewildered, on the bank of Lethe
He waits, his heart calls like a child in fear,
Calls out for me, who always answered.
If I had gone before him into hell
He would have followed, wilfuller than fate.
The swan-like woman, our own mother, and the swan-bright sire
Dowered us both with cold white hardihood,
But him with the wild swan's burden and perfection
Of single love. He needed me in life,
And, O, in death, implacable and holy sire,
His need is infinite, and tears my heart!
Let me cast off my youth, and die, and be with him!
I kneel for what men ask delaying of —
Beseech you, father, death!"
A great peace came, the stillness grew all peace;
The wings of the oak-trees drooped and curved themselves
Over the bowed young god. His bosom was drenched with peace.
And the glory of a voice bright-brimming

Covered him over with ravelled rainbows of music;
" As the wild swans beautiful and silver
Float in the coral air of summer evening,
Mated and inseparable lovers,
So I shall set the dear sons of the swan
In the low sky of summer, in the pure twilight,
Beautiful companions, silver stars!
Aldebaran shall call to them
And Sirius lift his blue targe in salute;
Orion's hail shall shake his jewelled corselet
And the young keepers of the outposts
Pacing the battlements and watch-paths of creation
Pause and turn on them their eyes, friendly and pure.
What sons of earth dare the vast floor of ocean
At sight of them, on evenings of early summer,
Standing together in dewfall, in the burnished twilight,
Shall dance on the deck and tipple the bulging goatskin,
For starlight weathers are at hand."
And Pollux heard; the tears broke;
He stretched himself on the ground,
And touched with his fingers the dark hem of the god.

A REGRET

That all my songs are sung into the air,
Like the rich-throated trees', unlistened to,
Would cost me but a summer-cloud of care
    Except for you.

But you, whom time is beckoning, would go
More happily if garlands you could see
Laid at my feet; which I'd at yours bestow
    How happily.

TYPE NOTE

This book is set in Electra, a Linotype face designed by W. A. Dwiggins. This type is not based on any historical model, nor does it echo any particular period or style. It avoids the extreme contrast between "thick" and "thin" elements that mark most "modern" faces, and attempts to give a feeling of fluidity, power, and speed.

The book was composed, printed, and bound by The Plimpton Press, Norwood, Massachusetts. The typography and binding design are by W. A. Dwiggins.